GW00458456

JUST A KIND WORD

JUST A KIND WORD

A life spent trying to uncover the truth

SHIRLEY DAVIES

HISTORY INTO PRINT

First published by
History Into Print, 56 Alcester Road,
Studley, Warwickshire B80 7LG in 2015
www.history-into-print.com

© Shirley Davies 2015

All rights reserved.

ISBN: 978-1-85858-348-8

The moral right of the author has been asserted.

A Cataloguing in Publication Record
for this title is available from the British Library.

Typeset in Baskerville
Printed in Great Britain by
by 4edge Ltd.

Contents

Dedication

This book is dedicated to:

Keith, who suffered the pain with me. Karen, Gail and Joann who made the pain easier to bear.

"Hindsight is the most wonderful gift"

Now in my eightieth year, I have made up for the unhappy days and count my blessings.

Acknowledgements

I thank
Keith's loving family.
Colin and Margaret.
My Grandma Winchurch.
Uncle Jack and Aunty Eileen.
Aunt Lily, Margaret
and Uncle Phil.

The Teachers at Mount Pleasant Junior School and Tipton Grammar School.
The few close friends that knew my plight and tried to help.

Chapter 1

One thing I know for sure is that during 1933 my father James Winchurch, married my mother Alice Baker at Christ Church, Coseley. There were no photographs to my knowledge and the ceremony was never mentioned again. They purchased a newly built semi-detached property in Ivy House Lane, Coseley which they named Kerwyn and established their home. Adjoining the property was a piece of land, which my father purchased and he had a small factory built then set up a wholesale sweet manufacturing business. The Winchurch family were all self-employed. James's parents had a thriving grocery shop nearby in Webb Street, his brother Jack was a wholesale tobacconist and later his sister Lily established a grocery business at Woodcross, Coseley.

Alice Baker, my mother, was from Ladymoor near to Bilston and was from a very large family. Indeed, twenty-two children had been born to her parents, Ellen and Robert, but only eleven had survived into adulthood. They were known locally as "the Baker's dozen" and they supported each other through thick and thin, never accepting outsiders. Robert predeceased Ellen by several years, then she died in 1938. I can just remember my maternal grandmother and visiting her at her home Peacehaven in Summerhill, Coseley.

I was born on March 3rd 1935 and my mother constantly reminded me of my difficult birth and the cost of her attendance at The Rosemary Ednam Maternity Hospital, Dudley, formerly Dudley Workhouse. As the years rolled on she added "It happened once between your father and me and you were the result." I was to be an only child.

I remember quite vividly my bedroom at Kerwyn, it was small and painted in pale turquoise emulsion, with pictures from "The Woman's Journal" that made a frieze below the picture rail. I had a straw cot with a fixed hood which I

My father's van. This picture shows my father on the left – but my mother is not there. I estimate the picture to be prior to 1928.

outgrew, I recall pushing a hole through the end with my feet and touching the cold wall. I also remember crying into the pillow and wetting the mattress.

My father was very busy with both his business and making improvements to the house. He soon added a full width veranda to the back with tubular heaters, a sunken well for the doormat and lighting. This extension added considerable extra living space and it also meant that the one and only toilet was accessible under cover. The original design of the property meant that the toilet, although within the curtilage of the house, was approached from outside.

Then followed work on the garden. It was a sloping site which he landscaped to provide a lawn, a rockery, steps and four rose beds that surrounded an ornamental pond. He used natural stone and created toadstools, raised beds and curving walls. The front garden was equally impressive and our neighbours must have been astounded by his workmanship as well as the cost of the materials, the other properties just had lawns with flowerbeds or chicken coops. I recall being able to carry just one house brick from the pile in the factory yard, to help build the veranda.

During this time, we had a visit from my mother's brother Bob with his wife Eve and their four year old son, Robin. Bob had attended Bilston College of Art, from where he had won a scholarship to The Royal College of Art in London. While a student he had met Eve, also an artist, and they married in London. Bob never returned to his native Black Country and his sisters openly said that when Eve married Bob, she had a meal ticket for life. So I saw Eve and Bob when I was four and would not see them again until I was in my sixties. I never saw Robin again but I do remember him peeing into the drain of our new veranda.

None of my father's family ever came to visit or even to admire the work that he had done to the house. However, my mother's sisters Maude and Bertha were constantly around. Maude was married to Jack Smout and they lived on the Birmingham New Road, at Lanesfield. Maude was an agent for Spirella corsets and measured ladies in the front room. Jack was a quiet, unassuming fellow who did as he was told and he worked at the Cannon. When the war began he was called up and was in the Royal Air Force. I liked Uncle Jack. He bought me my first Rupert annual, took me to see the Wolves play at Molineux, gave me a large bag of foreign stamps for my meagre album and an RAF propeller brooch, which I still have. Maude and Jack had no children. My mother said that Maude had lost

My father in 1928.

*My paternal
grandparents
Edwin and
Gertrude
Winchurch.*

My mother Alice.

My father Jim, 1932.

a baby because their little terrier dog had pulled on the lead while out walking. Later, Maude and Jack adopted two unrelated boys, when just weeks old.

Bertha was the youngest of the Baker family. She lived with Maude when the family home was sold upon the death of their mother and she also worked in the offices at the Cannon. While Jack was in the war, the two sisters lived together and Maude went to work at the Cannon doing Jack's work in accounts, keeping his job open until he returned. More of these sisters later, they could be unbelievably cruel and bitter.

Just before the war began in September 1939 my father became ill, as a teenager he had had rheumatic fever which had damaged his heart. As a family of three we went for a holiday to Hampton Loade in Shropshire and stayed with a family named Gwilt, they were known to my grandparents through business interests. My father had a car, indeed he had always had a car since a young man and a van for his business. I cannot recall much about this holiday, except that we spent a lot of time sitting by the river, sometimes crossing it using the manual ferry. Every morning Mrs Gwilt came to the bedroom with a huge jug of hot water, poured it into a large, pretty bowl and we used the water for washing. The house smelt of paraffin as there was no electricity and outside there was a huge fir tree within which, on wet days, Mrs Gwilt dried her washing.

Back at Ivy House Lane, life became very unsettled. I do not think that this was solely related to family matters or my father's failing health, the war was looming and people were afraid of the unknown. My parents were churchgoers, my father had been a longstanding chorister at Christ Church and the Bakers had attended the mission church of St Oswald in Ladymoor. So it was not out of the ordinary on Sunday 3rd September 1939 when my mother took me to Coseley Church for the eleven o'clock service. It was here that the congregation heard war had been declared. It meant little to me at the time, we walked home and presumably had our lunch.

My mother was not a good cook, nothing was measured, it was very much hit and miss so when food rationing began she had a good excuse for presenting a scratch meal. Puddings were mainly boiled rice with a blob of jam and main courses were usually stews and frequently included rabbit.

Although my mother was not an ambitious cook, she was an accomplished needlewoman. Leaving school at thirteen, she was apprenticed to a milliner and upon completion of her time began work at F.W Cook in High Street, Dudley.

This was a family business, selling high-class furniture, fabrics, haberdashery, clothing and hats. Upon her marriage she left Cooks and was presented with a chiming clock as a wedding present, it never kept the time or chimed accurately so it sat at the back of the sideboard for many years. Another wedding present, very inappropriate, was a statue of a nude lady and this stood to the left of the clock, dangerously close to the light switch and was damaged and repaired many times, until the inevitable happened and it crashed to the floor in the late fifties.

Much of the furniture for Kerwyn was purchased from Beachs in Bilston. I can remember two chunky armchairs being delivered 'on appro', one was blue and the other was fawn uncut moquette. The fawn one was selected, the matching chair and settee delivered and the blue chair went back to the shop. There was an oak dining suite, with four leather-seated chairs and a range of rugs. In the living room, where the dining suite stood there was also a leatherette sofa and one matching chair. There was a lot of furniture in the two reception rooms, with homemade pouffes, a dinner wagon, china cabinet and standard lamp. How do I recall this so clearly? Well at the age of nine, it was my job to do all the dusting and vacuuming. We had a vacuum cleaner called a 'Bustler' and I knew it very well. My father made a tall table that stood behind a chair and upon which stood the radio. You did not move the radio. Regularly, I took the accumulator to Millards Hardware shop to have it charged.

Chapter 2

Just after the war was declared, we went to stay with Aunt Louisa, who was a local midwife and her husband William Hambleton. They lived most comfortably in the Manifold Valley in Staffordshire, near to Butterton. Aunt Maude and Uncle Jack came with us and we travelled to Leek by train and were met at the station by William. I can recall the long drive up a hill into Leek. In 1992 we had a holiday close to Leek and I went to search for the station, only to find that there was a supermarket on the site but remnants of a wall remained.

William and Louisa's home Clayton House was palatial, I just loved it. This was as well because I was left to entertain myself for long periods, the six adults did not need me. However, I was so happy to spend time in the library, William told me how to get the books from the upper shelves by using a ladder and within the library there was a fine collection of clockwork musical instruments, which I was allowed to wind and listen to. I was in my seventh heaven. William also had a study and outside the door was an impressive trunk inscribed with his initials.

There was one very frightening area of the house, it was the room where I had to sleep on the first floor and to get to it I had to pass the narrower stairs to the attic. Within the room was a four-poster bed, accessed by wooden steps and if I needed the toilet, I had to lift the bottom step and there was a chamber pot. I was not yet five so before I went to get into this huge bed, Aunt Louisa warmed it with a copper warming pan as I watched and wondered if the bed would set on fire. "Jump in" she said and I can still recall its cosiness.

There were days when we all went out together into the pretty Manifold Valley. William had had a section of the river that was within his land, deepened so that he could take an early morning swim. We walked to the old track bed of the Manifold railway and came to a closed tunnel, William said that it was to be a storage depot for ammunition that would be used in the war. Today the tunnel is open to vehicles and walkers again, but there is no railway.

One day we went into Butterton to visit William's mother. Her house was covered in ivy, dark inside and full of old furniture, she was dressed in a long, fussy black dress. I cannot recall being given anything to eat or drink. Aunt Louisa had crocheted a pair of purple gloves for the local farmer's daughter who was getting married and she took me with her to give them to the bride-to-be. One evening we all went to the barn to see and listen to the barn owl, it was all so different from life in Coseley.

Soon after this stay at Clayton House my father developed pneumonia. This was a very sad time for me, as he was so weak. There were endless arguments about his treatment because he had changed his doctor from the well-known Dr Waddell in Coseley to an Indian doctor Dr Fozdar from Bilston and seemingly all the treatment offered was challenged. When a huge cylinder of oxygen was delivered to his bedroom, I became afraid. I knew that my father was ill because the bedroom fire was lit, it did not depend upon the temperature to have a fire in your bedroom, more on your health. The room was so full of furniture that even as a five year old, I knew that the bedspread was far too near to the grate to be safe. To add to the problem Maude and Bertha were frequently visiting my mother giving advice and causing yet more arguments. Miraculously, my father recovered. His own family did not visit him during his illness.

At four years old, I had my tonsils removed at the Royal Hospital in Wolverhampton. I clearly recall awaking from the anaesthetic and feeling the feet of another person in the bed. We had been put top and tail in an adult's bed. I believe that this was to get as many childrens operations done before the onset of war. I came home the same day and relished the jelly and ice cream menu for several days. Following on from this operation, I had an abscess on my neck which was treated with Kaolin poultices. I must have been rather run down because I returned to The Royal for a course of sunray treatment where several children sat on a circular bench facing a glowing pole, we turned our backs to the pole after a certain amount of time and were dressed in just our knickers.

On my fifth birthday, seven months into the war, my mother stood me inside the gateway at Kerwyn without explanation. My grandparents (my father's parents) drove to the gate, my grandma got out of the car and put me inside, before getting back in. Granddad drove to Birmingham and I was taken into a shop where grandma bought me a new dress. It was pink and deeply smocked. I wore it. Then we went into a jeweller's and I had a gold signet ring, I watched my initials being engraved upon it. Then I wore it. Our next visit was to a photographer's where I was photographed in my new dress and showed off my ring. We went to Barrows for lunch before returning to Coseley. As we neared Ivy House Lane, granddad stopped the car and my grandma put on my original clothes, the pink dress went into its bag. The car stopped outside Kerwyn, my grandma put me safely inside the gate and my grandparents drove away.

I started in the Infants at Mount Pleasant School, which was just about two hundred yards from my home, I had to cross the Birmingham New Road that had only been open to traffic for about five years. I was told to watch out for the convoys, these were lines of army vehicles moving men and supplies to wherever they needed to be. As I waited to cross the road by the Ivy House pub, I could see as far as Shaw Road and this was my guide to the time that I needed to get across safely. I feel sure that I was taken to school in the first few weeks but I cannot remember it.

My first teacher was Miss Snead. The desks were green and there was a swing tied to a bar in the ceiling. The windows were too high for me to see outside. I cannot recall learning anything but I must have done. We played with a few toys every Friday afternoon and I walked home at lunchtime.

One day the headmaster, Mr Stan Grange came into Miss Snead's lesson and told us to listen carefully. He held up a large sign and said that if we came to school and saw this sign hanging on the gate, we were to go to the air raid shelters. Before I left Mount Pleasant School in July 1946 I learned that the sign said 'PROCEED TO THE AIR RAID SHELTERS'. We did use the air raid shelters a few times, they had been dug out on land behind the houses in Ivy House Lane and we crossed the road to reach them. They were fitted with benches and while in the shelters we sang songs and recited our times tables. There were candles in red metal lanterns to provide us with light. I cannot remember if there were any toilet facilities.

I went home for my lunch one day to find much activity on the spare piece of land adjoining Kerwyn in front of dad's factory. They were starting to build a public air raid shelter, for fifty people! My father reckoned that he knew nothing about this plan, when he inquired he was told that it had to be built there and he would receive a peppercorn rent for the duration of the war.

My 5th birthday wearing the pink dress.

Arriving home on another day for lunch, I stood watching the builders digging deep foundations. Suddenly there was a bang as one of the labourers struck an electricity cable and was killed before my eyes.

I moved up to Mrs Pearson's class where the desks were yellow and I could not understand why the class library books were on a window ledge that I could not reach. My father made some amazing toys for me, I had a little theatre complete with battery operated foot lights and a drop down curtain. He made a desk, using conduit for the legs and lino on the sloping writing surface. Other toys were bought for me by my paternal grandparents. The Baker family did not indulge in gifts of any description.

Walking to see my grandma one afternoon, I met Nurse Prout the District Nurse who told me as she hopped off her bicycle, that she had left my birthday present with grandma. It was the A.A. Milne book "Now we are Six", it is still in my possession, rather battered and coloured in with wax crayons.

The war really began to impact upon our lives. Bombing of the Black Country was almost nightly, the targets were the engineering and steel works particularly Stewarts and Lloyds of Bilston. We seemed to spend most nights in the air raid shelter or hibernating beneath the stairs. As the pantry was under the stairs and off the small kitchen this was convenient, we had food to hand and the ability to use the Cannon gas stove. To ensure that no electric light could be seen from outside, my father made a plywood shutter that fixed into slots on the outside of the window frame. It was one of my jobs to put up the shutter as darkness fell.

Food rationing was not a serious problem to us as my grandma kept a very busy grocery shop. We lodged our three ration books with her as registered customers, as was the law and every Friday evening we went to grandma's to buy the limited groceries... tea, sugar, butter, margarine, all written in a small notebook. The list of groceries never filled the page. My father seldom came with us because he was by this time so frail that my mother and I walked to get the groceries, a distance of half a mile. However, it seemed a long way to me, especially carrying the groceries home.

My father's mother, Gertrude Cotterrill, was one of three sisters and had been born in Coseley in 1885. Her mother had a grocery shop in Fullwood's End, which she had prudently established in the front room of her home, the door of which opened straight onto the footpath. This was common practice, it was an easy way to set up your own business and presumably if trade was not good you re-established your room and recreated the parlour. On her 21st birthday, in 1906, Gertrude Cotterrill married Edwin Winchurch at Old Meeting Unitarian Chapel in Old Meeting Road, Coseley, opposite to the Clayton Playing Field. History repeated itself and her mother set her up with a few groceries, enabling Gertrude to establish her own shop at 38 Webb Street, Coseley, earning money that went into the household kitty. The property was double fronted within a row of small houses, overshadowed by Green's Foundry. As I write this, I can still recall the foundry smell.

Edwin and Gertrude had three children and Edwin was employed at the Cannon like so many men in the area. During the First World War business must have been good as my grandfather left his employment at the Cannon to work in the family business. He delivered groceries and looked after the heavier side of what needed to be done at the shop. When the war ended in 1918, plans were made to have a purpose built shop and family home built on a plot of land further down from the original home in Webb Street. It is this shop that I can remember.

I was their first grandchild, born to their eldest son James (Jim). Their other son, Jack, had established a thriving wholesale tobacco business, serving local shops and public houses in the wider Coseley area. Their only daughter Lily had married Bert and with the support of her mother rented a new Coseley District Council purpose-built shop with living accommodation, at the newly built Woodcross Estate in Coseley. The Winchurch family were all self-employed and all this had happened by the time I was born.

When the Second World War began, life moved on apace. The new purpose built house with shop and four bedrooms, was used by the extended family. The garden at 42 Webb Street had been well designed with a tennis court, ornamental pond, no less than four garages, a yard for parking and loading vehicles, raised beds of natural stone, shrubs, trees, water features and the very necessary wash house (the brew house a.k.a the Bruce). It must have been an amazing property to the locals in Webb Street, who were still living in back to backs, with outside taps and indescribable toilets.

In 1940 the tennis court was excavated and a brick built underground air raid shelter was created. It had a well fitted family room, cooking facilities and a good stock of food.... from the shop, of course. The entrance steps were by a Lilac tree, good camouflage I suspect and there was an escape route at the far end, via a ladder and through a manhole cover, back into the garden. I can recall trying to run up the high piles of soil from the excavation work before it was removed elsewhere. We did use the shelter and I remember it as a happy place, with lots going on.

In the shop, on the customers' side, the counter was about eighteen inches wide and quite high. Beneath this ledge, grandma kept the bread. It opened out to a lower, wider counter on the shop side, where grandma collected the customers' orders. Beneath the counter were huge drawers, one held all the grease proof and brown paper bags. In spite of sweets being rationed, there were always several jars at the back of the shop window display and I quickly became an expert in being able to open the screw top jars quietly to help myself to a sweet. Grandma must have seen me do this but I was never reprimanded.

The shop never opened on Sundays and every Thursday afternoon it closed at 1.00pm. But apart from that it was always busy and my grandma was very enterprising. She made lots of bread pudding using leftover unsold bread, made and supplied to her daily by Tilley's bakery in Wallbrook. The pudding was always ready, warm from the oven, when the men in the nearby foundries took a break. One man would come down to buy pieces for the others and I remember how dirty, from their work these men were. Women also came, usually with an enamelled jug and bought faggots with gravy. These were made from left over meats and offal, supplied and delivered by Devis of Dudley. These women were always friendly but seemed so weary and worn, one that I especially recall was Dolly, others were only known to me by their married names, Mrs Morris, Mrs Steed and so on.

Grandma was able to accurately cut lumps of butter, margarine or lard from huge blocks that sat on white enamelled trays, marked with the appropriate product name on the front. She was always able to find me a little job, I became good at bagging up sugar into 1lb blue bags from a huge sack and Friday evenings after supper were spent counting the food ration coupons and separating them into different 'Victory V' tins, lined up on the kitchen table. These were then taken to the food office, situated at Roseville House off Ivy House Lane and then grandma would be allowed further rationed food to sell to her registered customers. During the war, you had to register with a shopkeeper and that ensured that you received your quota of rationed food and all was fair, but that did not stop the black market.

Grandma treated her customers well and she paid for an outing by coach, to places like Walsall Illuminations, once a year. These outings were on Thursday evenings, when it would be dark for the lights to be at their best and as the shop was closed on Thursday afternoons so there was time for the family to set to in the kitchen and make sandwiches for the trip. She provided a drink and some times a caddy of tea as an extra "thank you".

The shop was kept well stocked, large hams covered in muslin hung from hooks in the ceiling and grandma would slice off rashers on the bone using a huge knife, while wedging the ham between her arms and her generous bosom (do remember that she always wore a clean apron daily!). The bacon slicer terrified me, probably because I had been threatened to keep away from it. Large cards hung from the shelving on which were stuck weird tins of Indian Cerete, Zubes, bandages, pens, pencils (carrying the Utility mark), Aspros and raspberry vinegar. Most of the shelves carried tinned food, simple plain stuff like processed peas, carrots, sardines, pilchards, the occasional tin of salmon and sometimes tins of fruit. Most of the food had the price printed on the label and there was a fine glass display cabinet at the end of the counter that advertised Cadbury's Chocolate, but it always seemed to house wool. As you left the kitchen to go into the shop, there was a large trap door in the floor that could be lifted up and this was the entrance to the huge cellar, I always crossed it with caution and I never ever went down into the cellar.

As the bombs rained down on the Black Country we just had to get on with our lives. I can never understand why so few children from the area were evacuated, it was such a dangerous place at that time.

My grandparents had a large circle of friends and they held regular Bridge evenings on Thursdays, of course. Among the players were: Mr Greensill, headmaster of The Manor School; the Revd George Garnham, Vicar of Coseley and the Tilleys, bakers from Wallbrook. It was prudent to befriend the Tilleys as they could cook your Christmas turkey in their large ovens. It was mainly the men that I recall playing cards, their wives sat in another room. Mrs Greensill would unravel her husband's worn out pullovers and reknit them into socks, what thrift! Mrs Garnham sat elegantly and talked. Other visitors I remember were the Walletts and the Rowleys, they were wholesale potato merchants in Bilston. But my favourite was Nurse Prout, she had treated grandma at home for some reason withheld from me. One time it was all planned that I should go to stay overnight with Nurse Prout in her accommodation at Bayer Hall and I was all in favour. However, when I saw the bedroom I changed my mind and was adamant I had to go home. Nurse Prout walked me back to Ivy House Lane, annoyed, I would imagine.

The grocery business did well due to long hours of hard work. Everyday grandma wore her clean, white, wrap around apron, laundered on Mondays by Mrs Holmes who lived nearby in Foundry Street. I stood and observed her hands on washing days, they reminded me of the chitterlings that grandma sold in the shop... all wrinkled and white. On her belt, grandma had a heavy bunch of keys and one of them opened the safe covered with a lace cloth that stood by her bed. From an early age, I recall thanking her for the large white paper £5 note that she would give to me before a holiday or an event at school. As an extra to this, from the age of ten, grandma gave me half a crown pocket money every week. I did not realise its value at the time, but I never wasted it because I loved books and would go to Hatchards bookshop that was within Beatties in Wolverhampton, to buy the latest Enid Blyton or any other book that caught my eye.

My grandparents had an Austin Six motorcar, registration AJW 845, we still have my grandfather's battery charger and they had a telephone, Bilston 42139. The house was furnished with beautiful cut glass, fine carpets and a piano. It was warm, welcoming and always busy. Grandma was widowed on Boxing Day in 1943. I could not understand as a child, why her beloved Ned had to die at Christmas and it seemed to ruin Christmas for everyone, forever after.

I remember spending many nights in the air shelter with my father present. It was, to a small child, good fun and if the air raids went on for a long time, you knew that school was optional the next day. One night, my mother refused to go into the shelter until she had washed my hair with Durbac soap because I had nits. This caused all sorts of fiery comments but my mother said "If she is going to heaven tonight, she is going with clean hair!" Another refuge was in the cellars of a property owned by my grandparents, it had been a public house called The Bull's Head but had been turned into a cluster of small homes. In the cellars there were arches where the barrels would have stood and they made ideal cubicles for individual sleeping areas, giving a little privacy. I recall it as a cold place to spend the night and it was open to anyone but most of the others who sheltered there were customers of the shop. There was one particularly coarse man who would come down the stone steps chuntering "Aye it a gaem, aye it's a bloody gaem". He was told directly to curb his tongue as there were children around.

At home we had an Anderson air raid shelter set below ground in the piece of wasteland in front of the sweet factory. As the land was clay soil, invariably the shelter was full of water and debris. On one occasion we did go into the Anderson shelter of our elderly neighbours, Mr and Mrs Hughes, I never heard them called by their first names. The air raid siren sounded and off we trooped into the Hughes' shelter. There were five of us sitting on the wooden benches, awaiting Mrs Hughes. She was late. When she did arrive, she was dressed in her fur coat and carried a black tin box, her Deed Box. Anxious to get her inside, Mr Hughes sighed with relief when at last she was with her family, within the shelter. "If I am going to meet my maker tonight," she said, "I will be wearing decent clothes, just look at you lot in your tatters."

We did almost meet our maker that night, a bomb was dropped on the Birmingham New Road, some 50 yards from where we were sheltering. When the all clear siren sounded, we walked with crowds of others to view the damage. Unlike Mrs Hughes, most people were in nightwear, siren suits, or old clothes. As I stood among the crowd, I thought that it looked like a scene from the Bible. Having viewed the damaged road, we walked home to see our own house. All the veranda glass was shattered, a bedroom ceiling was down and there was brick dust everywhere. On another occasion, there was a direct hit on the new public house at the bottom of Ivy House Lane, the Horse and Jockey. It was said that the bomb fell onto a metal beam which diffused it and no one was injured. The publicans, Mr and Mrs Bishton were able to take a few days off while the damage was cleared and admitted that they were happy to do so.

One morning, while I was still in Miss Pearson's class, she announced that Frank, a boy in our class had been killed by a bomb which had fallen near to Vicarage Road. We sat and stared at the empty seat by the yellow desk, seemingly unaffected by the tragedy.

The outbreak of war prevented my father continuing with his wholesale sweet manufacturing as sugar was rationed and so were sweets. He closed the business and took employment, first with Thomas Perry in Bilston and later a lighter job with an electrical company in Dudley by the name of Bunce. He was provided with a car and probably because he was less stressed, having no business to run, he seemed to enjoy better health. He became an ARP Warden for our section of the lane.

Moving into Miss Stant's Class at Mount Pleasant, I was now in the Junior School. Sometimes my grandfather would collect me from school at the end of the day in his Austin Six. My grandfather, my father and Uncle Jack always had motorcars. This caused problems when other children teased me and I remember asking him to park a little further along Mount Pleasant Street, thinking that I would not be seen riding in a rather large motorcar. He did not. I remember him clearly even though he died in 1943, when I would have been just eight.

There were to be no more holidays because of the hostilities and travel only when necessary. Petrol was rationed, road signs were removed and street lighting was off. There was a war on and we all had to make an effort and sacrifices, as children we knew things were difficult. I do not know why I was not evacuated.

It was while I was in Miss Stant's class that my older cousin Bertha decided to join the WRENs. Bertha was the daughter of my mother's sister Sally who had married Bert Ward. He had no credence in the eyes of the Baker sisters, but neither did any of the other in-laws, as they repeatedly said "He is not of our flesh and blood." Cousin Bertha had a clear out of her clothes prior to enlisting and one day she arrived at our house with a bag of second hand clothes for me, I was about seven and she must have been seventeen! Some days later I was told to wear one of these items of clothing, a pink woollen jumper, heavily matted under the arms. I knew that I did not perspire to that extent! My mother had made me a grey pleated skirt from an old pair of men's trousers, so I had a new outfit and set off for school. Sitting at my desk, I felt ill at ease, the jumper was awful. I did not put up my hand to answer any questions because of the matting under the arms. It was torture for me. At the end of the day, when we had said our prayers for the Lord to keep us from harm and safely through another night, Miss Stant dismissed the class, but she called me back and asked what the matter was, I had been so quiet all day and had not taken any part in the lessons. At first I denied that anything was amiss but she continued to question me until I cried and admitted that it was all because of the pink jumper and showed her the problem. At this, she dismounted from her high chair, gave me a hug and sent me on my way. Arriving home, I put the jumper in the dustbin. Nothing more was said and I cannot remember what happened to the rest of Bertha's hand me downs.

I remember enjoying being able to read and asking for books. At this time there was no library in Coseley and to travel to Dudley or Wolverhampton was unthinkable. Fortunately, Mr and Mrs Hughes, who lived next door had some books in their front room and I did my best to pay them regular visits. At home we only had a war atlas, a dictionary, hymn books and a bible or two but we did take the Radio Times weekly and I had my "Sunny Stories".

I loved to watch Mrs Hughes bake cakes and she always let me scrape the mixing bowl, telling me that raw cake mix would give me worms and I often fell asleep on her sofa. The best thing about visiting next door was being able to look at the books, there was a complete set of Charles Dickens, other lighter novels, picture books and sheet music, because they had a piano. I wanted a piano more than anything else, Mrs Hughes never said that I could touch their piano and I did not have the courage to ask if I could. Her house was always tidy and warm, she was excessively house proud and just as particular with her appearance (remember how she dressed for the air raid shelter?). Each evening when Mr Hughes and their son Fred returned from their jobs at a factory, their meal was set in a scrupulously clean shed. They would then change from their working clothes before going into the house. They kept chickens in a coop in the garden but let them forage in the adjoining fields.

Chapter 3

I remember the wonderful games that we played in the fields, although they were not actually fields but redundant coal pit banks. They were uneven, grassy and littered with coal slag and pit shafts, indeed a fantastic adventure playground! The area was bordered by 1930s houses, roads and the Birmingham canal, with the added attraction of the Coseley tunnel, lit by gas and the very first canal with a towpath on both sides. I loved the pit banks but was terrified of the tunnel. Many people close by used it as an air raid shelter, they even left bedding on the towpath in readiness. I was always reminded that if I had nits in my hair I would be dragged to the water under the tunnel and many children were made to walk through the tunnel as a cure for whooping cough.

On the pit banks we made dens, created a rodeo using old bikes, lit fire cans, went into what we called caves and pretended to be Cowboys and Indians. We were very dirty at the end of a good day's play. There were only two girls and probably five boys, all of similar age, who could access this dream play area as we lived in the newly built houses.

One day we built a superb den, it took all day. We had dragged wood, old sheets and bits of furniture to create this dream and then we decided that we would sleep in it overnight. My mother refused to let me be part of the plan so I walked home to sulk and went to bed. I was up very early the next day to get back to the action. I looked from my parents' bedroom window and saw the police and gypsy horses at the den. I dressed, went outside like a shot, through the gate onto the banks. Apparently, during the night the gypsy horses had circled around the den in curiosity and in so doing had broken through an iron plate that had been placed over a pit shaft, the boys had spent time dropping bricks down the hole to discover the depth. One of the boys, Ray, went to tell his father who had come home from a night shift and Mr Goodall seeing the problem called the police. It took Coseley Council weeks to fill in the shaft with rubbish from the dustbin collection.

We had hours of fun and freedom "over the banks". As children we were sent to fill buckets with coal from the redundant pits and during the severe winter of 1946 you had to fill the bucket, no excuses, whatever the weather, life was tough for everyone. The only flowers to grow on the pit banks were coltsfoot and rosebay willowherb. Gypsy horses roamed freely, although they were tethered by long lengths of oily boat rope.

Finally the war in Europe ended in May 1945. This was a time for momentous yet controlled celebrations, there were street parties and special church services to help people feel that life would now improve but the country was in a huge amount of debt and there was so much damage to repair.

I really wanted a bicycle but knew that this was not possible. Most of my friends had one and I had a scooter but it was not like owning a bike! One day my friend Audrey said that she was having a new bike for her combined birthday and Christmas present so when the new bike arrived, she would sell me her old one. This was a dream come true. I was able to buy the said bike for half a crown. It was only a 24-inch wheel and would not last me long, but it was a bike and I could get around easier and quicker. The bike needed attention and help came in the form of the curate of Christ Church, Coseley, the Revd Enser. He offered to paint the bike for me. Little did I realise how long it would take him to keep his promise, so I pestered and pestered him, calling at his house and asking his daughter if the bike was ready. Eventually, it was and I collected it. The black glossy paint was still wet in places and by the time I had ridden it home, I had paint on my clothes and on myself. However, I left it to dry for a day or two and realised it needed a few bits and pieces to improve it. I then had a stroke of luck. I found a ten shilling note, damp but undamaged in the grass by the Anderson shelter. I knew this was on our land so considered the money to be mine. I went into the village, where there was a cycle shop and spent the money on brake blocks, new rubber pedals, a saddle and a little saddlebag. The man in the shop fitted all the new bits onto the bike for me. I rode home so proud of my bike that had cost me just 12 shillings and six pence. I then worried about what my mother would say, surely she would ask me how I had paid for these extras but she did not and I kept my lucky find to myself. Audrey and I enjoyed some fine cycle rides together.

I spent every Sunday going to church, sometimes I attended all three services. Audrey came with me but we had to walk on Sundays, bikes were not allowed. Sunday School was in the afternoon and led by Miss Burton. We were not at all well behaved. Looking back, I am sorry that we gave her such grief when she was giving up her afternoon for us. Each time we went to Sunday School, we had a stamp for our special album, I missed one Sunday and did not receive my stamp, this spoilt my attendance record and I was cross. However on the following Sunday, when the stamps were given out, I noticed that the stamps for the previous week were still in the tin. At an appropriate moment, I managed to steal one and add it to my album, it was only when I left church to go home that I felt guilty. I still have my Sunday School stamp albums and I always attended well enough to get an annual award, usually a book that was unsuitable. I can remember just one that I actually read "Ronnie and the Creed". When we left church after Sunday School, there would be families gathering by the West door for Christenings. The babies' mothers always looked so ill that I decided that having a baby was not for me.

My mother was keen for me to succeed and for several months prior to sitting the 11+ examination, I had tuition from a friend of my Uncle Bob, Andrew Barnett, who taught at a Coseley school. Mr Grange, the Headmaster of Mount Pleasant Junior School called a small group of eleven year olds into his room and told us that we had passed the 11+ examination, "Run home and tell your parents." I ran down Ivy House Lane, across the Birmingham New Road, watching for the Army convoys, as I had been told. It was sometime later that my parents received confirmation in writing.

My first choice was Bilston Girls' High School and on Empire Day, May 24th 1946 I went for an interview. I travelled on a single decker Midland Red bus, from Millards the ironmongers in Coseley, all the way to Bilston. My mother came with me and I was encouraged to remember the cost of the fare, the distance and the time it took, also that it was Empire Day - all the pink areas on the maps in the atlas!

Waterloo Road, Bilston seemed endless. Then an imposing brick building came into view, Bilston Girls' High School (BGHS), the grounds beyond the gates seemed to roll on forever. There were cars in the driveway near to the main entrance. Mount Pleasant School did not have a drive and I cannot recall any teacher having a car, at any rate not at school.

My mother and I were met at the door and asked to wait in a room close by. I was most uncomfortable in my home made tweed coat and matching bonnet style hat, the terror of the situation still haunts me. Within a short time I was ushered into the Headmistress's study, my voice seemed to fail, my thoughts seemed muddled and when the final question was posed, my mind went blank "Please tell me the time by the clock on the wall," said the Headmistress. It had Roman numerals, I lost any concentration that I had and mumbled something approximate. "You need to be more accurate than that," I was told and she had obviously made up her mind that I was not suitable to wear the green and grey uniform. When she said that I could now leave I walked to the heavy door, struggled with the knob, finally the door opened and with a sigh of relief I left.

My mother did her best to convince me that I had done alright, but I knew better, after all I had been in the interview. We walked together down the drive, crossed the Wellington Road and called at my uncle's house, number 172. Waiting there was not only a cup of tea but a bundle of second-hand BGHS green and grey uniforms that had belonged to my cousins. My heart sank.

My final weeks at Mount Pleasant were filled by washing out ink pots, usually filled with blotting paper, then refilling them when Mr Williams had made more ink from powder in a tin. I also became good at arranging flowers in jam jars. As I feared BGHS did not want me, I had at the age of eleven, been rejected.

There seemed to be lots of adults talking about me but not to me. Then I was told that I had another interview at the newly created Tipton County Grammar School the very next week. The journey this time was on two Midland Red buses, the 125 and the 244. Throughout the bus journey my mother continuously prompted me with facts and how to cope with the interview, "Say that you want to be a teacher," she insisted, "you need a grammar school education for that." As we approached Locarno Road, I became quite excited by a large brick building that I thought was the grammar school, it was not! The bus continued to Alexandra Road, where we alighted. No long drive, no imposing gates, just a single storey brick building. We sat in a small foyer off the cloakroom with other children and their mothers, in 1946 fathers did not seem to be on the scene in the day-time. I was feeling a little more at ease for this interview, having insisted upon leaving my tweed bonnet at home, after all I had two lovely plaits of thick brown hair.

I went into Mrs Graham's room, she was an elderly lady, kind and gentle. I recall swinging my legs as I sat on the chair and noticing the pattern on the rug beneath me. I can not remember any of the questions, only her smiling face. When the interview was over she said, "Thank you, Shirley, you may leave now." I opened her door with ease. Away we went to wait for the red double decker and my mother asked "Did you tell Mrs Graham that you wanted to be a teacher?" I really did not know what I had said but it must have suited Mrs Graham because she accepted me.

I left Mount Pleasant School, where under the guidance of some sound teaching, I had learned my arithmetical tables, spellings and grammar, together with lots of songs, mainly in the air-raid shelters. Even after 64 years I can still remember lots of the names of other children in my class.

During the Summer holiday I had to gather my new school uniform. The blue cotton blouses were made by my mother from material purchased from Hawkin's in Dudley. The navy blue box pleated tunic and the gabardine mac were bought. A family friend knitted the cardigan and my mother knitted the black stockings, which were never long enough and very itchy. An aunt bought my black shoes in Shrewsbury and someone gave me a beret. The war had only been over for a year and everything was still in short supply. My grandma bought me a leather satchel that lasted for seven years, then my bus pass arrived and I was raring to go.

The school bus from Dudley was always packed, boys upstairs, girls downstairs. Hats and caps to be worn at all times, no eating in the streets and always offer your seat to adults - all done without question. The camber on the canal bridge in Owen Street, Tipton always caused the bus to rock a little, occasionally helped along by us pupils! The level crossing at the end of Owen Street caused us to be late on many occasions, it all added to the excitement of the journey to school.

Some sixty girls assembled on the first day, from as far apart as Wednesfield and Brierley Hill. Looking back, I believe that the Education Committee of the time realising that there were insufficient grammar school places, quickly upgraded Tipton Central School, something that could not happen so quickly today.

There were two forms of 30 girls for all lessons. Cookery and Needlecraft were taught for the first two years and I still have the embroidered cover that I made for my hymn book, indeed I still have the book too, perhaps I should have handed it in when I left!

Latin was introduced and a Library was created in Miss Cansdale's room (was she really related to George Cansdale from *Blue Peter*?). We were taught by some very fine ladies with the highest standards: Miss Kathleen Titley, who introduced us to Shakespeare and Wordsworth; Miss Roberts, with her upright back, pretty face and iron discipline, taught History (and improved my handwriting) and Miss Hamilton-Roberts, who taught Biology in a laboratory that was most inadequate. The Biology lab and the Needlework room also doubled up as the Dining Room each day when the dinner ladies brought in the canisters of hot food and served it to us. The menus were less than thrilling! Miss Sherwood tried to teach us Maths, she was so able, she could not appreciate our difficulties and consequently we made life in the class-room difficult for her and were later very sorry. Miss Davies taught Art and Dancing, always wearing her blue crepe soled sandals, they must have been old as crepe soles were not available during the war. We danced to a wind-up gramophone, perched on the edge of the stage, the winding up being done by girls who were "un-well". Miss Davies was understanding, she knew everyone's monthly cycle, you could not fool her, making excuses for forgetting your shorts, aertex or pumps!

All girls had to have a wash bag that hung on their coat peg, in it was a towel, soap and a nailbrush. Hands had to be washed before lunch and the Prefects saw this happen. We paid 2½d per week for our daily 1/3 pint of milk, later it became free. So 30 bottles of milk were delivered to the classroom at morning recess, punched and a straw inserted, if you drank it slowly it would last all through break and you would not have to go outside, a good ploy on a cold day. I think that a school meal cost 9 pence a day.

The playground was small for 320 pupils, with a tennis court overlapping a netball court, confusing enough but an added complication was a large drain cover somewhere near the centre. Aiming for the drain cover always troubled the opposition, when playing matches. Beyond the playground was a large but poorly maintained sports field used mainly by the boys, for football and cricket. It had a thin covering of grass, quickly worn down to black ash and I clearly remember the clouds of dust that were created. Between the playground and the field, were the air-raid shelters and it was here that the bravest girls went to meet the boys at lunch-time (one such young man, I have been married to for 57 years!).

Looking back, I believe that we were encouraged to make the most of our opportunities at Tipton Girls' School, by today's values the facilities were poor but the standards set were very high. We enjoyed annual drama productions, educational visits even to Paris in 1948 and after the GCE examinations we were taken to The Festival of Britain in 1951. I longed to see my name on the impressive Honours Board on the rear wall of the Hall but I never did, no one seemed to keep it up-to-date. However, I do still have my school prizes signed by Miss Farrington and Mr Philpott for various subjects. After my A levels, in 1953 I went to train as a teacher, keeping my promise to Mrs Graham, who had faith in me at the age of eleven and the school motto 'Loyalty' has always been useful to me.

My father died on March 15th 1947 in his fortieth year and from then on life became hard for me because my mother made me feel that I was a burden and there were so many rows and fallouts between her, my grandma and her sisters, especially Maude and Bertha.

The day that my father died, I remember so well. He was in bed with an oxygen cylinder by his side and when I left my bedroom to go downstairs he called to me to give him a kiss, I had thought that he was asleep but he heard me and called. I gave him the kiss and told him that I was off to get the meat, as it was Saturday, it was the weekend joint, meat was rationed and the joints were small. I set off for my grandma's shop, she was busy and I pottered about for a while, then I went into the shop to see what was going on and a lady came in and said "Mrs Winchurch, your son Jim has just died." Jim, my father. It hadn't been that long since I had kissed him goodbye before setting off. I would never see him again. Grandma took me out of the shop and into the kitchen, sat me down and gave me brandy. I was too distressed to cry. Aunt Lily was kind to me, she had lost her brother, grandma had lost her eldest son. We all mourned together.

Communications were not easy in 1947, grandma had a phone for the business but there wasn't one at my home, however things seemed to move quickly. Soon to arrive at Webb Street was Mrs Garnham, the vicar's wife, a friend of my grandma. I was taken to Coseley Vicarage, treated to all kinds of niceties and a lovely tea, then I was shown to a room and gathered the intention was for me to stay at the vicarage overnight. I was not happy about this and recall being difficult, so much so the vicar put me in his car and took me home. Aunt Bertha was there with my mother. There were no words of comfort or reassurance, nothing. A bed was made up for me in the box room as my mother and Bertha were using my bedroom. My father was laid out in his bedroom and stayed there until the funeral.

On Monday 17th March 1947 I set off to catch my buses to school with a note to let them know that my father had died. I gave it to Miss Hamilton-Roberts and she put it in the Register. I got on with the day. I did not go to the funeral. I cannot remember what happened to me on that day.

Chapter 4

From then onwards my life became very difficult. My mother had a serious fallout with my father's family, I lay on the settle in grandma's kitchen crying, listening to tirades of abuse from my mother. The outcome was that my mother took our ration books from grandma and she re-registered us with her sister Sally, who kept a grocery shop in Bradley.

This was yet another job for me. Each week I had to take the grocery order to Aunt Sally's in order for her son Grenville to deliver the order on a Friday evening to Ivy House Lane. It was a mile from home to Aunt Sally's so my bike was invaluable, even if it was now too small for me.

In spite of the rift, I continued to visit my grandma. She gave me half a crown for pocket money each week as well as other little treats. For my birthday she bought me a budgerigar, complete with cage and the necessary toys to entertain the bird. Aunt Maude called a few days later, not with a present for me, that was not her style, looking at the bird in its cage she said "It'll be dead in a week." The very next morning, it died. Grandma replaced it for me.

While I was at Mount Pleasant School and the war raged, I often went with my grandma to Birmingham. She bought goods for her customers at a variety of warehouses Lunts, Bell and Nicholson's or Wilkinson and Ridell's. We ate at Barrows, every time we did these trips travelling by bus. When I started Grammar School I could not go to Birmingham with her in the week because the school was stricter about attendance, the war was over and so there were no excuses about being bombed out.

But there was one special outing. Grandma took my cousin Margaret and me to the Ideal Home Exhibition at Olympia. We travelled by coach to London and we were allowed to see the exhibition on our own, providing that we reported on the hour beneath a clock, grandma and her friend would meet us there. We never did the recce and managed to survive the day eating free samples of food and drink. My school accepted the reason for my absence because I had been to London.

Aunt Lizzie, another of my mother's sisters had married Philip and they had a son, Graham, who was two years older than I was. Uncle Phil initially had a good haulage business in Woodseaves, Staffordshire with his brothers. When the haulage industry was nationalised, they sold the business and he invested in a farm at nearby Norbury. This meant that they left their semi-detached house in the village and moved into the beautiful Blakemore House Farm. I had spent several holidays at the little house in Norbury, I remember going along the lanes picking blackberries that Aunt Lizzie would cook. There was no mains water laid to the

Margaret and Shirley visiting 'The Ideal Home Exhibition' in 1952 with grandma.

house and so drinking water had to be collected in large, unspillable cans from a spring in the grass verge. I could only carry half a can, Graham could cope with a full one.

Aunt Lizzie had a daily milk round and driving a small van, she collected two and a half churns of milk from a nearby farm. When I stayed with her, she took me on the milk round and I quickly learned how to pour milk from a small can into the jug that was left on the doorstep. If it was a Friday, I even collected

With my cousin Graham, Norbury, 1937.

the money. There was much to do but there was always an element of fun. I watched in awe as Uncle Phil dug a well in the garden and bricked it down to the watercourse once this was in use there was no need to get water from the spring at the roadside and life became easier.

Once when I was staying with Aunt Lizzie she noticed that I had a wart on my finger, giving me a small piece of raw meat, she advised me to rub it on the wart and then bury the meat in the garden, I did just as I was told and kept the burial spot to myself. The wart vanished within days. Aunt Lizzie had a series of evacuees living with them and there were also Italian prisoners of war working in the village, so it was all fascinating and exciting for me. I was still able to stay when they moved to Blakemore House Farm. There was, however, one very serious drawback to this property, the 'bucket and chuck-it' toilet that was outside, it always seemed full to the brim and smelly.

Busy as he was, Uncle Phil always had time for me. When I off loaded my concerns about being too big for my second-hand bike he had a proposal, "You save for a new bike and I will match your savings, pound for pound." What an offer that was!

Chapter 5

Back at Ivy House Lane, my mother had found a position at an exclusive leather goods shop in Wolverhampton called Hudson's. She worked every Saturday and I was left to my own devices so long as her tea was on the table for 6 o'clock. She stayed at Hudson's for a short time, until she was approached by her old firm, F.W Cook of Dudley to return to the Millinery department. This was more to her liking and she made the move, which was to be her life for the next twenty years, until she retired in her early sixties.

Familiar with the set up and knowing the people that she worked for, she was happy and had an income. Benefits were not the order of the day in 1947, but she had 8 shillings a week for me, her widow's pension and the warehouse that my father had built for his business. This had been rented to an engineering company for a few years and the income helped to pay off the mortgages for the warehouse and the house. My mother was in a strong position for a woman of those times and she also enjoyed good health. At the time I was unaware that she was not declaring the income from the factory rent to the tax office and in later years she was made to repay the unpaid tax, which resulted in her being on Tax Code 0 for several years. I believe that had she not had the responsibility of me, the consequences of her action would have been much more severe.

Work became her sole purpose in life and soon after her appointment, she rose to be the millinery buyer and enjoyed visiting fashion houses in London. Many of her evenings were spent creating special headpieces for wealthy clients and she specialised in weddings. She was able to buy costumes (suits in today's parlance) combined with blouses and expensive shoes that she wore for work. As soon as she came home, she changed into old clothes.

As her life-style improved, from having had a very frail, sick husband for almost five years, mine deteriorated. The amount of work that I was expected to do grew daily. The housework was my responsibility and occupied all Saturday morning. The rear garden was also my job, my mother did the front garden because she could be seen by the neighbours. I had to do all my own washing and ironing, sometimes with some bits of my mother's. There was only a gas fired boiler in the outside shed and water to this boiler had to come from the kitchen tap, by a hose-pipe through the window, across the path into the wooden shed. It was no wonder that I did my washing by hand. Tablecloths and sheets went to the laundry on a monthly basis.

I would get home from school at five o'clock, there was no heating and so my first job was to light a fire using a gas poker, it was so cold that I kept on my school gabardine mac until the room warmed. Then I had to cook tea for us, which had to be ready when my mother came home from work. Daily, I pleaded with her to clear the table after breakfast, because I left the house at eight o'clock and she left forty minutes later. She never did. Washing up to her was a chore that was for me.

My only respite was on Wednesdays, when it was her half day. All towns had an early closing day, Dudley's was Wednesday. Usually when I got home, either Bertha or Maude were with her, tea was a stew in the pressure cooker and the washing up was still there for me, there were also the cups and saucers from the afternoon tea party. In spite of all these jobs, I managed to keep up with my school homework, except when it came to reading, if my mother saw me with a book she would announce, "I can find you something better to do than that."

Saturdays were a problem. I was on my own after the housework was done so sometimes I had to go to meet my Aunts Maude and Bertha as they left work at the Cannon Office and I went with them to Maude's house at Lanesfield, Coseley. It was a new house, larger than ours with a hall and more efficient kitchen. After a bite to eat the sisters set about doing their washing in the kitchen using a dolly tub and a mangle, which stood near to the sink and they would find a job for me too. I was delegated to turn the handle of the mangle and while this was going on they entertained me, singing hymns. Sometimes I stayed overnight but usually at about five-thirty I walked home to be there, with the kettle on when my mother returned from work.

We spent Saturday evenings listening to the radio. Occasionally we were visited by my mother's brother, Alfred, he came on his bike bringing us a few home grown vegetables and he brought a touch of relief to the long silences that occurred when it was just my mother and me. Alfred was married to Sarah and they had six children, his sisters referred to Sarah as "a slut", they did not appreciate that their brother was part of the reason that there were so many children to look after! Another brother, John and his wife Sarah had four children and lived on Wellington Road, Bilston, this Sarah was referred to by his sisters as "Sarah, the dozy", but to me as I was growing up, she seemed a most refined lady.

To help resolve the problem of what to do with a twelve year old girl on Saturdays when her mother was working, Aunt Maude made me a junior member of the Cannon Tennis Club, she was a player and I was able to go along to play and meet others. I enjoyed this new horizon. I also spent time on Saturdays at grandma's, although the shop was open, it was less busy and she had time for me. Aunt Lily was also there with my cousins Margaret and David. The Webb Street garden was large and well maintained, there were four garages and a warehouse that was used by Uncle Jack, who was a wholesale tobacconist. When he was busy putting up orders, Margaret and I helped him, collecting cigars, cigarettes, snuff and tobacco from the racks of shelving. I can remember the smell of that warehouse to this day. Margaret was four years younger than I but we got on well together. In the winter Aunt Lily would bank up the open fire in the lounge where we played saying, "Watch out you lot, I'll roast you!" There was a piano in the lounge that added to our amusement, as did the sandwiches and grandma's victoria sponge.

In 1948, there was a school visit to Paris during the summer holiday. Surprisingly, when I took the details home my mother said that I could go. The cost was £40 for the week inclusive, and I would also need some new clothes. My grandma gave me some money, relieving my mother of the total cost. While I was in France, my mother went on a coach tour of Scotland, she also bought herself a new gold watch. The benefits of working full time were becoming apparent. I just hoped that she would be happier and kinder to me.

In the summer of 1948, after the visit to Paris, I was back to filling my days before the start of the new term. I cycled to Clayton Playing Fields, Coseley and joined a small group of others killing time, like me. We were a mixed bunch. One boy had a large bag of boiled sweets and was handing them around. It was the start of a change to my life. The following day, we congregated at the playing field again, the boy with the sweets was named Keith and said that he went to

Tipton Grammar School and lived in Pemberton Road with his brother Colin. Initially I refused to believe him and we had a little confrontation, then the rest of the group dared us to go into the nearby air raid shelter and have a kiss... we did!

For a week of the Summer holiday, my mother was asked to go to Wellington to look after her sister Florence's baby linen shop while she and her husband Percy were taking their annual holiday in Bournemouth. We went to Wellington by train, I liked this town and spent most of my time wandering around the shops. There was a very small WH Smiths, I would sit on the floor reading books that I could not afford to buy and no one came to move me on. Woolworth's was also very appealing with so many small items to see in the divided counters.

I then discovered Currys, where as a manager's special, there was a full sized bike, second-hand in excellent condition for eight pounds. My Uncle Phil's offer sprang to mind, I already had four pounds so I needed to contact him at once. This was easily done because Aunt Floss had a phone and I rang the farm to speak to Uncle Phil, he was his jovial self, remembered his promise and said that he would send the four pounds. Meanwhile, he suggested that I asked my mother to lend me the cash. We went to Currys, explaining who we were to the manager, he knew my aunt as a local businesswoman. The almost new bike was mine! I took it back to Coseley in the guards van of the train to Bilston and then I cycled home from there hoping that someone that I knew would see me, but it was not to be. I was in my element and decided that on fine days I would cycle to school, I did have a free bus pass as I lived more than three miles from school, so I could use the bus in bad weather. My old and too small half-a-crown bike I gave away.

Chapter 6

I think that I became a bit of a burden to Aunt Maude at the Cannon Tennis Club. To be fair, she was considering adopting two children and realised that her time for tennis would be limited. She said that it would be better for me to join Coseley Athletic Club next season, where tennis and cricket were played seriously and she would help me join. She kept her promise and duly paid ten shillings for me to become a member of the Tennis Section. It was to be a good move, there were more activities and plenty of young people. We could buy our tea on a Saturday, which really was the left over food from the cricketers' tea, they did not leave much but Mrs Callaghan the volunteer caterer, ensured that we had the crusts off the loaves dipped in tomato juice with added salt and pepper... delicious and for only six pence!

I still spent a lot of time with my grandma, she was obviously concerned for me, knowing what my mother was capable of doing. When my father died, grandma had offered to pay for me to go to the Royal Wolverhampton School but my mother was adamant that I should stay with her and would not allow me go as a weekly boarder. I suppose that as I was now at Tipton Grammar School I did have the same advantage, but being a boarder would have saved me from so many domestic chores and sadly, the more proficient that I became at these jobs the more came my way. I could not win.

I attended Church regularly and I heard that there was going to be a religious production just before Christmas. I auditioned for a part and got that of the Narrator. There were pages to learn and some of it I failed to understand but I was word perfect by the time of the dress rehearsal. Then came a big disappointment, I was to wear a long black cassock. There had been far too much black in my life already and this was so upsetting. Church or no church, I would not be wearing black. To enable the rehearsal to begin, I took my place on the temporary staging in the church and gave it my very best, just to prove that I was a necessary player in the production but I would not wear black. When rehearsal was over everyone walked home, parents at that time did not pick their children up, so nothing was said and I was not asked how the rehearsal had gone.

The following Wednesday when I came in from school, there sat the Vicar with my mother. It was her half day off from Cook's, "What's this all about Shirley? You spoilt the rehearsal on Sunday, I hear." I drew myself up to my highest point and said, "I will not wear black." There was some cajoling but I refused to change my mind and suggested that they offered the part to someone else. This was my trump card. I did want to perform but on my terms and I knew it would be impossible for someone else to learn the part in the time left before the performance. The Revd Garnham finished his cup of tea and left, it was all still in the balance. When, three days later it came to the actual performance, waiting for me was a bright red cassock which I wore and stepped confidently onto the stage.

Chapter 7

Playing tennis regularly improved my game, I was never too keen on sport before because of the energy I had to find to complete the long list of jobs that I had to do for my mother. I got on well with the other junior players, between us we went to several different schools and we always had lots to discuss. The boy with the sweets was a member too.

At home, one Saturday morning, as I was carrying out my jobs I had a visit from Maggie Fownes, a senior member of the Tennis Club. She was on her Raleigh ladies bike that had a dress guard over the rear mudguard (my Aunt Maude had the same model). Standing on the doorstep, she asked me if I would play in the Junior Team match that very afternoon. I was so pleased to say, "Yes, thank you Mrs Fownes." Away she rode. I then realised what I had done, I had white pumps that were cleaned ready to play, a white cardigan, but no white dress. Normally I was allowed to play in my school PE kit, which was navy and pale blue. I had to act quickly. I went to the airing cupboard and found a heavy white cotton sheet. To cut the story short, at 2 o'clock I was ready and waiting to start my very first game for Coseley Athletic Club Juniors. I was wearing a white sleeveless dress, with a dropped waistline and little pleats. I cannot remember whether we won or lost, but it had all been a challenge to me and I had triumphed. But I could not change my routine and I pedalled back to Ivy House Lane, to ensure that my mother's tea was on the table when she came from work. I told her about my extraordinary day, she listened, chastised me for cutting up the sheet and pushed me up to bed. I cried myself to sleep.

The following day at Church, no one looking at her could ever have imagined how she treated me, her behaviour was nothing short of exemplary. I was the one with a secret that I could not tell anyone.

My mother did have a friend who was kind to me, Mrs Caddick or Gertie, she lived nearby in Langley Avenue and called most Saturday evenings because, although she had a husband and two children, she was on her own a lot. She was kind and generous with the little that she had. On very cold winter days, she would go to our house after lunch and light the fire for me, so that there was some warmth when I returned from school, she knew where the key was kept and it was a little secret between her and me, I loved the days when she lit the fire. I was always so hungry at five o'clock when I came home from school, my favourite snack was to have toast with lard, sprinkled with salt. Biscuits were not often purchased.

The very worst scenario was to come home from school to see half a ton of coal tipped on the pavement in front of the house. I had to cart it in buckets, as we did not have a barrow, to the coalhouse behind the shed, it was dirty and tiring work. I needed my mother to say, "Thank you, you have done well" but no, she took everything for granted and expected me to do all this for my "keep".

One Saturday in July playing tennis having broken up from school, Keith told me that he was going on holiday with his family to Llandudno. "My mother is taking me there too, we could meet up," I said. We arranged to be on the Prom at eight o'clock on the Saturday evening. It worked! We made the necessary introductions and as we all came from Coseley, it was agreed that we should meet again the next day. It worked well, there was Keith's mother and father, his Aunty Olive, his brother Colin and his girlfriend Jane. We all paired up beautifully and the week for me was the best ever.

Back at Coseley, there was the rest of the Summer holiday to fill. My Aunt Lily took Margaret, David and me to Blackpool for a few days, we travelled in a new Austin Cambridge and came home via the Mersey Tunnel. Grandma had given us all a white £5 note and we used them to buy tickets for shows at the Tower. I returned to school in September 1949 ready for my third year, with an eye on the exams in two years time. I was able to take part in productions, which I enjoyed and the rehearsals were after school.

With Keith in Llandudno 1948.

With my mother in Llandudno.

With Keith at Weston-Super-Mare.

*Keith with his Auntie Olive and the
Staffordshire Bull Terrier puppies
– bred by his father, Fred.*

With Rose at Weston-Super-Mare.

Since spending time in Llandudno, Keith and I became good friends. We often cycled to school together. He invited me to his birthday party and I was stunned by the kindness within his home, everyone was welcome with food and drink readily available and you did not have to get them yourself, you certainly did not have to wash-up. It was all so comfortable. Grandma's house was welcoming but there was always the business creating activity, it was never quiet there. My home was well furnished and maintained but it always had a cold atmosphere that was not welcoming. There was little that I could do about it. I tried to make my bedroom cosy but had limited success. I just had to make the best of life.

After several years having had no contact with my father's family, my mother made the first approach to heal the rift. I have no idea why, but she did. It made me happy and she went out and about with Aunt Lily and Aunty Eileen, Uncle Jack's wife. The counter side was that my mother fell out with Maude over her adopted boys. There was never a time when she was happy with everyone.

In my teens, I had a nice cluster of friends including Margaret Smailes, who later became my sister-in-law and after Evensong on Sundays we went back to someone's home for tea and biscuits and if there was a record player, listened to music.

My mother and I had holidays in Ilfracombe and Folkestone (when my cousin Margaret came too), I was always pleased when we met someone who would tag on to us, to help with the conversation, as a holiday with my mother was difficult for me. We travelled by train and changing for Ilfracombe, I noticed a religious bill poster, "Come unto me all who are heavily laden, and I will refresh you"..... I took that personally.

For a short time, my mother left F.W Cook, this again was because of falling out with colleagues. Eventually she returned to Cooks and stayed until she retired. My mother never gave me any encouragement or praise. I found out from her friends, that she told them what a good girl I was but these remarks were less than comforting to me, I still felt like her lackey and at times looked like one. She had no idea how to offer a treat or console, whatever she did for me was done for her benefit. People told her how marvellous she was, doing what she did for me, a big girl, still at school, not earning her keep, "Alice you are wonderful" rang in her ears and made her swell with pride. I set my sights on some good exam results that would enable me to leave home, I had endured enough. It was only because of my grandma, Keith, his family and my friends that I kept buoyant, spending more and more time away from my home.

I made most of my own clothes. I knitted and embroidered and to make a bit of pocket money I made circular skirts for friends. Grandma was still giving me pocket money and buying extras. She bought me a Biro for my birthday, I used it to complete some History homework that I thought was very good. Two days afterwards, Miss Roberts called me to her room and asked what I had used to write the work.

"My Biro, Miss Roberts."

"Show it to me." I fetched it from my form room and Miss Roberts used it to scribble on a piece of paper but said nothing. The next day in assembly we were told 'ALL BIROS ARE BANNED'. I had the only one, thanks to my go-ahead grandma. She also bought me a Dunlop tennis racquet, a silver Yard-o-Lead pencil and a Waterman fountain pen.

How I kept up with my schoolwork, I do not know. I was taking the maximum eight GCEs and had all the domestic jobs, the shopping, the rear garden, the washing and most of the cooking, except Sunday lunch. I was determined to get to college and become a teacher.

I had much support from Keith's family from the age of fifteen, every Saturday when I had done my jobs, I put a plate and some cutlery in the kitchen sink and added water, and this stopped my mother asking me where I had had my lunch. I changed for tennis and then rode to Pemberton Road, where there was always a cooked lunch waiting at Keith's house. After lunch we went to Coseley Athletic Club to play tennis, Keith's father followed later to watch the cricket, this was routine during the summer and was a delight for me. I still had to be home to have my mother's tea ready for six o'clock.

Keith was made welcome at grandma's but my mother was not so easily won over. Until she had a problem with the floor in the bay window, it had gone rotten and Keith's father said that he would replace it for her. The necessary certificate was granted to obtain the tongue and grooved flooring and Keith and his father did the job. This kindness improved the friendship with Keith's family and my mother was often invited for tea on a Saturday, after work. There were untold kindnesses, which helped me to cope with my mother, in hindsight, I believe that they were done to help me. Many people knew how abrasive she could be and how harshly she treated me behind closed doors.

Chapter 8

In June 1951, Keith and I sat the very first GCEs that replaced the Matriculation Exams. We enjoyed the summer holidays playing tennis, borrowing Colin's tandem to cycle to Sutton Park and sometimes going out on the bus. When the exam results came, we had both done well enough to return to school in September and join Sixth Form.

We added to our interests by joining the Wolverhampton Literary Society and benefited from the monthly meetings. Often Keith's Aunty Olive gave us the money to go to the Clifton Cinema in Coseley, which was in walking distance and Keith played a lot of badminton. It was easier to manage schoolwork with fewer subjects but we only went out on Thursday evenings and Saturdays.

My mother became more embittered as I grew older and I began to fight my own corner and tried to stand up to her abuse but not only did she have her own strength but also her sisters Maude and Bertha loved to hear about our confrontations from her and added their unbalanced views.

Maude and Jack had adopted the two baby boys which my mother was totally against and frequently said so, she referred to Roy and Graham as "the adopted ones", Maude called them "her angels". Then for some unknown reason, they became friends again and we paid them a visit. In the corner of the room was a large object covered by a cloth. "What's under there?" asked my mother. "A television," replied Maude. The cloth was pulled off and a wooden cabinet with a small screen was exposed, all was explained and we were invited to call again on a certain day to watch the opening ceremony of Sutton Coldfield transmitter, which we did and I remember it well. Of course, we had to watch it with the curtains drawn.

Bertha had married Bill and they lived with his parents in a terraced house in Bloomfield, Tipton. Within months, they moved to the adjoining house and stayed there for years until re-housed in a maisonette that was not too far away.

They had no children. Indeed, the six Baker daughters only had five children between them and the two boys adopted by Maude and Jack. Bertha was easier to get along with and had a dry sense of humour. Bill worked all his life at The Bean Factory in Tipton. He was fussy, never held an opinion, was overly generous, never owned so much as a spanner, never drove a car and spent all his holidays with Bertha, at Morecombe Bay. Later in my teaching career, I often spoke about my Uncle Bill in assembly, he was "a non-person" and I encouraged pupils to become involved in life and love all it has to offer.

My mother took great pride in reminding Bertha that she was the only one in the family in rented accommodation. They argued about everything, whether at our house or at the maisonette. My mother was 91 when I took her to visit Bertha for the last time, Bill had died a few years previously. I read the newspaper, sitting on the red leatherette sofa, as they argued bitterly. Bertha had prepaid for her funeral and my mother was totally against such a "stupid thing", she also reminded Bertha that she did not have much to leave anyway. Driving my mother back to Ivy House Lane, I told her that I would never take her to see Bertha again and have to spend my time embarrassed behind a newspaper. Her reply was "Well, I am right", she was always right. Later, Bertha's death and funeral became the reason why I never saw my mother again.

The Prefects outing to The Festival of Britain in 1951, after the O Level exams. I am centre backrow – wearing gloves. I was suffering from my skin complaint again.

Chapter 9

At the beginning of the Upper Sixth, Keith and I began to consider which universities we should apply to for admission in October 1953. I wanted to teach and when I had to complete my applications for college courses, I needed my birth certificate. My mother told me that it was in the locked cupboard of the sideboard. I found it among other papers including my father's Last Will and Testament which I had never seen before. I was alone in the house, my mother was at work, when I read it and discovered that in 1947 my father had left me £100 for a piano, it was now 1952 and I had never been told about his bequest. He knew just how much I longed to play the piano. My mother had said nothing and never did. I kept it in mind until 1997, when provoked so much by her, I asked her why she had not respected my father's wishes. Her reply was "We were too poor." I knew that this was yet another lie, my father would not have left me money that he did not have, and the Winchurch family were never short of hard earned money.

Keith wanted a Physics Degree for industry and settled on the University of North Staffordshire (Keele). I had failed Latin and at most universities it was a requirement so I was delighted to have an unconditional offer from The City of Worcester Teacher Training College (University of Worcester) following a two-day interview. The offer gave me enormous peace of mind. In retrospect, I do wonder if my report from the grammar school related the multitude of problems that I had at home. Going to Worcester was wonderful, it changed my life in a way that I could never have imagined. I was free and could concentrate fully on my academic work.

Keith and I put a huge amount of time into getting the best A Level results to achieve our goals, it was a tough time. In June 1952, Keith passed his driving test at the first attempt and he persuaded his brother Colin to let him use his

Ford 8 to travel to school. We drove together, cap on and beret on, being careful not to break school rules. The next day we cycled and Keith was informed that arriving by car was not to be done on a regular basis. We could not anyway because Colin needed his car to get to work.

My mother still expected all my jobs to be done and they were, they had to be to keep some kind of peace within the house. I went regularly to see my grandma and enjoyed the treats she had for me and I still went to the weekend retreat at Hampton Loade as often as I could as Margaret and David, my cousins, would be there and it was good to be in a family situation and not be expected to do all the jobs. The adults did them not the children.

My father was never mentioned. I used to visit his grave after Sunday School and just stand by myself and think would my life be different if he were still alive? The Winchurchs were totally different to the Bakers. The Bakers only loved themselves. My father's grave never had a headstone, it still has no headstone. Grandma offered many times to provide one but this was refused by my mother and it caused yet more disagreements, everything seemed to start another row.

We left Tipton Grammar School in July 1953 aged 18. There were no regrets, we hoped that our efforts with A Levels would be worthy and they were. It was at this time we took stock of our long friendship and agreed that when we left Coseley to go our separate ways, should either of us meet anyone else, we would be fair, honest and move on.

During August, I went to have my usual break with Aunt Lizzie, Uncle Phil and Graham at the farm. Within days, Graham wanted me to go to the cinema with him in Newport and I was perfectly happy to go until I realised that he had affection for me, which I did not wish to encourage. He was my first cousin and I had always enjoyed his company so I was on dangerous ground. The next day, I asked if someone would take me back to Coseley and Aunt Lizzie did, I believe that she had some idea of why I needed to leave Blakemore House. I did not see much of Keith except at the Athletic Club and we were always with the crowd.

Chapter 10

Aunt Lily took my mother and me to Worcester where I bought my college blazer and scarf. I also purchased some of the books as grandma had given me money for these essentials.

I received a full grant from Staffordshire County Council of sixty pounds per annum. Because I was under twenty-one, this was paid to my mother and on alternate weeks she posted to me a pound note or a ten shilling note (50p) without fail. However, you do not need a Mathematics Degree to appreciate that an academic year consists of 36 weeks, which equals 9 months at £3 equals £36. She was up to her old tricks again. I knew that I could not question her and again relied on my grandma to help me financially and bless her, she did. What was happening to me, the eldest grandchild and only child of her son who had died at 39, must have been breaking her heart.

Worcester was wonderful. I could do all my work and I was only responsible for myself. I became involved in some of the many societies, my world expanded overnight and I met some amazing people. It turned my life around and gave me the confidence I needed. I revelled in the teaching practices, the course work, the debates, the late night discussions but above all else, my freedom. I went into Worcester and bought a pair of trousers, my mother would not allow me to wear trousers so I never took them home.

Throughout this time, Keith was doing well at Keele and we wrote to each other three times a week for four years. We met as usual during holidays and our friendship continued. My years at Worcester went all too quickly, I graduated surprisingly well and looked forward to beginning my teaching career at Albright Girls School in Oldbury.

My third teaching practice had been at Albright Girls School, I remember I went for a day to meet the Headmistress, Miss Elizabeth Drewry and the staff who would be guiding me and was given a timetable. Two weeks later with my lessons planned, I returned to do my best. It was an inspirational experience. Miss Drewry ran a very fine school, everyone worked hard and enjoyed a sense of achievement. There was a uniform of sorts, a white blouse, navy skirt and cardigan, with an optional tie. They were not from any particular outfitter in the town, they were acquired from wherever. The girls were all from loving, caring homes, with little money for extras. I enjoyed my teaching days, even though I was exhausted when the practice finished. Before I left on the Friday afternoon, Miss Drewry called me into her office and after a few words of advice, said that she would be able to offer me a teaching post the following year when I was qualified, I was very flattered.

I did my final teaching practice at a secondary school in Bridgnorth and when I completed my training decided that the right place for me was Albright Girls School. I contacted Miss Drewry and true to her word she said that she did have a post for me and if I wanted to teach for two weeks before the end of the Summer Term 1955, I could and I would be paid! I did not receive any holiday pay as my full-time contract would not begin until September 1st 1955.

September arrived and I was given my own form and was in at the deep end. There were other members of staff who had been trained at Worcester. Colleagues that I remember include: Elizabeth Smith (Modern Dance); Alice Lunt (English), she had written several books for children; Pauline Walliter (Science); Miss Boot; Mary Eccleshall; Tina Pine; Pam Samson and Mrs Gooch. There was also a science teacher who told me to eat a Marmite and margarine sandwich every day to keep fit. The small staff room was upstairs, the rest of the school was all on ground level, built around a quadrangle, within which there was a well kept lawn. There was an identical school for boys adjoining the girls' school but the twain never met.

Albright was surrounded by factories, BIP, Albright and Wilson, Accles and Pollock, Chance Glass to name a few. In warm weather it was not possible to have the classroom windows open as the air was so polluted. We suffered too from serious bouts of smog, I recall one afternoon in November when Miss Drewry called a special assembly at around two o'clock as the smog was so thick that the school was closing early indeed, immediately and we were to go straight home. I waited for a 74 bus on the Birmingham Road with a handkerchief tied around my mouth. No bus came. A person walking past and informed me that there would be no more, so I began to walk to Coseley. It took me so long I called to see two friends en-route. Eventually, I made it home but was exhausted. What I would have done to have had a mobile phone but we did not even have a phone at home.

The school had an apology for a sports ground, just a rough field to the rear of the site. Serious sporting events went on at local, well manicured Company sports grounds. The girls walked to the local park to use the hard tennis courts, an entire form of 30, with one teacher. On one occasion, a girl in my care fell heavily and seriously damaged her knee. I had to leave the girls, call at a house and phone for an ambulance.

Lunch was eaten in the Main Hall and was cooked in a kitchen at the Boys' school. The Staff sat on a raised platform at the end of the hall and there was an unbreakable rule, Miss Drewry sat at the head of the table and as other teachers came to have their lunch they had to sit by the next teacher, leaving no spaces or empty seats. Miss Drewry stayed as long as she wished and was not supposed to sit alone.

Every day there was an Assembly, taken by Miss Drewry. She was inspirational and full of enthusiasm, what she delivered in assembly lingered in your head all day. Every other year we held a Health and Beauty fortnight when each lesson had to have this as a theme. At sometime during the day, the bell would ring and everyone went to the hall. Miss Drewry, resplendent in one of her many costumes (a business suit in modern parlance) wearing a small corsage as ever, spoke to the gathered school, then would check the girls nails or shoes and socks or hair. She provided small prizes as rewards, with certificates and a grand assembly at the end of the event.

I believe that the girls benefited greatly from The Flat, an area the size of a classroom that had been divided into a hallway, a sitting room, a bedroom and a bathroom. Each week three girls spent each day together in the flat and "kept house". They had to work out a budget to cover the cost of their meals, snacks and a little for entertaining using their dinner money plus a subsidy from the school and were allowed to buy their food from a shop on the Birmingham Road where the shopkeeper was sympathetic. They planned menus, cooked the meals, did the necessary housework and entertained their friends and members of staff. Not only did the girls benefit from this experience, they simply loved it and left school at fifteen well equipped for the world of work.

I travelled to school by bus and Miss Drewry travelled by train from Stourbridge with Mary Eccleshall. She sometimes gathered a few pupils along with her as she walked from the station. I became adventurous and bought a Cyclemaster wheel for my bike but this form of transport was only for travelling in fine weather, all too often the sparking plug became clogged and the bike would refuse to go. All highly embarrassing, if the pupils were around.

At home one Sunday morning, my mother answered the door bell and there stood three pupils from my Form. "We have come to see Miss Winchurch" they said. My mother invited them inside, I went into the sitting room and could hardly believe my eyes "Why are you here, where should you be?" They had used their pocket money to travel on two buses to find me. They were given a drink of squash and then I escorted them to the bus stop for them to return to Oldbury. On the Monday morning I went directly to see Miss Drewry to tell her what had happened. As I expected, she understood. The girls were in school and nothing more was said. I did learn later that the girls had asked my mother if she was my housekeeper! At the time, I was only twenty-one.

I used several weekends to take my Form on walks to Kinver or Clent. We went by bus and took our picnic. The only money we used was to pay the fare. I do recall a girl named Jennifer, sitting beneath a tree, eating her picnic. She looked up into the tree and shouted at the birds, "SHURRUP, WILL YA!" We had fun.

At home during a Christmas holiday, I read with great pride that Elizabeth Drewry had been awarded the OBE for Services to Education. She deserved it. The day after she went to receive the award, she came to school in her finery, together with her bouquet of flowers. The pupils sat on the floor in the hall and eagerly listened to the story of her Investiture at Buckingham Palace. I don't think that there was a child in the school that had been to London. Indeed, I had only been twice. Once for The Festival of Britain in 1951.

So, Elizabeth Drewry, thank you for all that you did for me. Under your careful guidance, I really learned my trade. You taught me more than my teacher training course did and it stood me in good stead for forty years.

There is just one other memory to recall of this time. As we sat in the staff room one day, someone said, "They are going to build a road on stilts, at the end of the school field, according to the newspaper." "Don't be so ridiculous," was the curt response. When I use the M6 now I look across to the Albright Girls School site - happy days. Incidentally, my daughter currently attends meetings at Albright, although no longer a school, it is still an educational establishment.

In August 1955, I had been invited to join Keith's family to holiday in Minehead, together with Margaret, my old Sunday School friend, who was now Colin's girlfriend. I was planning to fund this holiday with money that I earned teaching at Albright for two weeks at the end of the Summer term, but my mother had other ideas. She took all that I had earned from me, I was devastated... it was my holiday money. I did have the holiday, courtesy of Keith's family who covered the cost. My mother never turned a hair.

I began to regret accepting Miss Drewry's offer of a teaching post and believed that I would be been better away from my mother, teaching somewhere else. I had hoped to save some money by living at home but in three years, I had saved £90. I cannot recall how much I earned. Whatever I bought my mother criticised, having my hair done was wasteful and considering an endowment was wrong and again I had her sisters Maude and Bertha adding their weight. Living at home was a mistake.

I had a Singer sewing machine on approval at home for a week, I used it, liked it and intended to buy it. However, returning home from teaching on a Wednesday, my mother's half day, to my horror the machine had gone. "I had it collected. You cannot afford it!" she roared. I had an Evening Class at Bilston Technical School on a Friday evening, the fees from which would have covered the cost of the machine. I began to realise that my mother was a damaged woman. I had no idea what had caused it and I certainly was not helping. Was she jealous of her only child?

I had to keep out of her way so I joined a cookery class with my cousin Margaret and a woodwork class with my old friend Audrey. I had my Evening Class at Bilston Tech and I went to my grandma's, Uncle Jack and Aunty Eileen's, and Keith's parents to be out of her way. The best weekends were the ones I spent at Keele with Keith.

The rows continued with everyone she came into contact with, except Keith's family they never retaliated to her contentious remarks which I believe annoyed her, but she could not fault their kindness.

Keith graduated from Keele with his BA Hons in the summer of 1957 and to celebrate we hired a boat on the River Thames for a week with two friends from Keele, Alan D and Alan F we had a marvellous time. I did not tell my mother until two days before we left for Bourne End to pick up 'Sunflare', she was not amused and accused me of "being up to no good" with three men, I was so upset by her attitude.

Keith had an unsuccessful interview with the RAF, then a successful one with Blackburn Aircraft in Brough, East Yorkshire. He found somewhere to live and began work in August 1957. The aim in those days was to earn, as a graduate £1,000 per year. I really missed him, he was so far away and in those days with no motorways and driving a homemade 'Forstin Special' it was too far to travel regularly from East Yorkshire to Coseley. I was happy to travel to see him by train and he lived with a fine, generous Yorkshire family, the Smiths and they made me welcome too. I loved their village lifestyle with folks popping in, fresh garden produce and beautifully cooked food. It was my perfect lifestyle.

Chapter 11

In January 1958 we decided to become engaged. When Keith asked my mother in the correct manner I could not believe how wild and angry she became, it could not have been a shock to her, we had been firm friends since the age of thirteen. Whatever she said made no difference and she must have realised that. She was exhausted after her tirade and when things calmed down, Keith left Kerwyn and I went to my bedroom.

We announced our engagement in the local paper and I chose a ring from another of Keith's Keele colleagues, whose father was a jeweller and lived at Henley-in-Arden. My mother then seemed to have second thoughts, "Shirley we need to ask Keith's family to come for a meal." I could not believe what I heard. No one had a meal at our house, just cups of Camp coffee or Barrington's tea, but if she was becoming a little more humble I had to co-operate. The invitations were given and I was instructed to sort out the said meal for the following Saturday night. We even had the fire lit in the front room, by me of course. My mother came home from Cook's and the gathering began with Fred, Rose, Olive, Colin, Margaret, Keith, my mother and me. We ate, had coffee, sat and talked but there was no mention of the engagement and before 9.30 the party was over. It was unbelievable.

Keith's family started to collect cutlery for us, Margaret and Colin gave us a piece of Poole pottery, Aunty Olive gave us some money and even the neighbours gave us useful presents. My mother gave us nothing. Keith returned to South Cave and I just had to cope. I should have realised that Maude and Bertha would have seen the announcement in the Express and Star. On the Monday evening, they arrived, "What's all this Alice?" I sat there as the three of them raged on. "Where has he got the money for a ring?", "Where are you going to live, my girl?" Just anywhere but near to you lot, I thought, the sooner we get away the better. In the midst of all the ranting, I left the room before I had to make them coffee. Aged twenty-two I sobbed myself to sleep. They were relentless in their insults, what did they all want? We were two young qualified people, who had a long-standing friendship and we knew that we wanted to marry. We would both be twenty-three when we married.

I really needed my friends now, I was in a pathetic state and suffered a recurrence of the blistering skin rash that affected my hands. I had suffered from this problem since the age of nine, Aunt Lily used to buy pure cotton gloves to protect my hands, my mother said that it was due to eating too many apples. In retrospect, it was nervous tension. I was unable to teach for a month before my skin healed. The tormenting from my mother, Maude and Bertha continued. Why did my mother support her sisters and not me?

Keith and I continued with our wedding plans and chose Swanage for our honeymoon, Keith had a special interest in the geology of the Jurassic coast. I did not care where we went, I just had to get away. Keith's mother made our three-tiered wedding cake which I decorated and I made dresses for my cousins Ann, Helen and Mary, who were going to be my bridesmaids, as well as my own dress. My mother expected me to choose the fabrics from F.W Cook's as she could claim her discount. She did not pay for as much as a reel of thread and while I sewed the dresses, my mother was completely disinterested. Within two years of the wedding, she he had used the pearl buttons from the dress, re-used the veil and cut pieces from the skirt.

One evening she produced a form for me to sign. It had a list of all the numbers of my National Savings Certificates that my father had bought for me and amounted to around sixty pounds. Initially I refused to sign it but she was so domineering that I gave in to her. A few weeks later she said that the wedding reception would be at The Station Hotel in Dudley and we were going to visit the following Wednesday to discuss the menu, I was to break my journey from Albright and join her. This I did.

I realised that my National Savings were going to pay for her idea of a smart wedding. Invitations were sent to her brothers and sisters, her brother John would be "giving me away" as she had fallen out with my father's brother Jack, again. It was better for me to fall in with her scheme of things and get the 26th July over. Keith's mother and father paid for the wedding service sheets so that we could choose the hymns and the service would be at ten o'clock at Christ Church in Coseley, where the Winchurch family regularly attended.

Frequently, my mother asked me if I really intended to go through with the wedding, she was also not happy that the date chosen was the start of the works holiday fortnight, it was not a good day, indeed common. I had no answer, I was exhausted. I was still doing the garden, the housework, teaching and planning our wedding. Keith was working in East Yorkshire and trying to find us somewhere to live. I had already applied for a teaching post at Greatfield High School in Kingston-upon-Hull and following a day-long interview was offered the post of Head of Textiles. At least some things were going well.

We married at Christ Church, Coseley, 26th July 1958.

Replies to the wedding invitations were slow to come in and by the deadline, none of my mother's family had replied, neither had my grandma, Uncle Bert, Aunt Lily, Margaret or David. The acceptances were from our own few friends. I let my mother deal with The Station Hotel about the numbers that they needed.

The big day dawned and it was raining. Aunty Eileen arrived with her three daughters, my bridesmaids. My bouquet was delivered from a Wolverhampton florist and Uncle John appeared. My mother said nothing as she got ready. I hoped that I looked my best but there were no kind comments or words of support from my mother, she would not even help me get into my wedding dress. It was Aunty Eileen who saw my distress and helped me put on my dress. As she left for the church with the bridesmaids my mother turned, looked me straight in the eye and said, "For God's sake don't get lumbered with a load of kids."

As I walked down the aisle, I noticed my grandma, my cousin Margaret and Aunt Lizzie in the congregation, which gave me a boost. Bertha, Maude, Sally and Floss were nowhere to be seen.

When the service was over, we drove to the reception. I spoke to a waiter and ensured that an extra place was set on the top table for my grandma and the other extra guests were fitted in elsewhere. After the speeches, we left the reception as planned at two o'clock in our precious MG which had been safely garaged at the hotel the previous evening to ensure that it was not decorated or damaged. We were on our way to Swanage, I was free from my mother's emotional abuse, anger and jealousy. But not forever.

Chapter 12

We had a fantastic week playing tennis, walking the cliff tops and looking for fossils. We were so happy, we regretted that we had waited a year after Keith graduated to be married. Hindsight is a wonderful gift!

Returning to Coseley, we waited a few days, packed the car and left for Hull, where we were renting part of a house on Boothferry Road. When we drove away from Coseley my mother went into one of her hysterical fits and said that Keith had taken from her all that she had - "her girl". Did she mean me?

We were so very content with our new independence, everyone was friendly and kind. I began my new teaching post and we spent time exploring East Yorkshire. We were close to the sea and wonderful countryside. We returned to Coseley during October half-term and stayed with my mother but shared our time by visiting grandma and enjoyed catching up with Keith's family. My mother reminded me that the rockery needed weeding and I managed to fit that job in before we returned to Hull.

Life was good for us and we were able to save a little. By mid November, we realised that I was pregnant and we would need to have our own house. We looked around and found a new build in the nearby village of Swanland, it would be ready at the end of May, six weeks before the baby was due. We had a good deposit, Keith's parents and Aunty Olive had given us very generous sums for wedding presents that we had invested. Keith and I were both extremely practical and knew that we would be in our element in a home of our own, our one concern was the overdraft that we needed to pay off on Keith's MG. Aunty Olive came to our rescue saying, "You two cannot afford a debt and a baby" so she settled our debt and never asked us to repay her.

We spent Christmas at Coseley, sharing our time and our news with everyone - we were buying a house and having a baby. There was one person who was not happy, my mother, "You two disgust me. With all your education, I'd have thought that you would have had more sense." There was no answer to that. "Anyway, I am too young to be called granny!" she shouted as she left the room.

Back in Yorkshire we returned to work, moved from the rented house into a flat on the foreshore at Hessle. At weekends we went to visit our new house in Swanland. We were so excited. I stopped working at the school at Easter and spent time making things for our new home and the baby. Keith's mother had lent me her sewing machine and I was in my element.

We moved into 5 Queensbury Way in May 1959 and our daughter Karen was born on 6th July, it had all worked out perfectly for us. Karen had to stay in Beverley Westwood Hospital for a month because she did not gain weight. In sheer frustration, Keith and I removed her from the hospital against the advice of the doctors and took her home. Our own doctor and the local midwife came to help us and with time and care, Karen began to thrive.

It was a very hot summer and we had many visitors, staying for weekends. Grandma came and brought boxes of tinned food from her grocery shop, a teddy bear for Karen and a shawl that she had crocheted. We had splendid retired neighbours in Queensbury Way, who were like adopted grandparents and our social life was good.

We spent Christmas 1959 at Coseley. We were just able to travel in the MG with the carrycot in the back and our luggage strapped on the rear rack. We waited for an appropriate moment, when everyone was at Keith's parents' house to announce that we were expecting another baby. After a moment of silence, my mother went ballistic, I was upset and embarrassed by her attitude. Keith's father Fred spoke up, "Alice, they need our support and not your sort of behaviour." But she would not be quiet and went on to tell us that we would end up in the gutter, breeding like rabbits. It was a good thing that we had pre-empted her reaction and chose the time to tell the news, we had already enjoyed a hearty tea and were ready to take baby Karen back to Ivy House Lane to put her to bed. We were pleased to be returning to Swanland.

Soon into the New Year, we realised that a second baby would limit our travelling in the beloved MG, there would be a need to change to another car and we decided that a Wolseley 1500 would be the best buy. We did much to the house and it seemed that every visitor came with useful gifts, Aunty Olive gave us money for carpets, Rose and Fred bought lovely clothes for Karen and we redeemed my teacher's superannuation and bought a garage (many years later I repaid this back into my pension pot and benefited greatly).

Karen was christened in the tiny chapel in Swanland, Colin was her Godfather and Aunty Olive, her Godmother. She was given silver cutlery, a rattle, spoon & pusher and a bracelet from Keith's family. My mother provided an old white towel that had been in the airing cupboard at Coseley from as far back as I could remember, it was one that I had embroidered with a red W in the border when aged about 15 and it had two rust marks. It reduced me to tears. Keith's family had even arranged my mother's transport to the Christening weekend. She had always told me how thrifty she was but it was mean to the point of being spiteful.

Keith's mother Rose came to stay a few days before our next child was due as I had decided to have a home birth, but the baby was late and Rose had to return to Coseley because she was going on holiday with Fred, Olive and my mother, they went to see the Passion play at Oberammergau. In spite of my mother's behaviour, Keith's family were always so kind to her.

The birth of our second daughter Gail made us a happy family of four, with a Wolseley 1500 and a cosy home with an unmade garden. That would be the next project. Our visits to Coseley became less frequent as we tended to set off to the seaside on Yorkshire's east coast.

Keith knew that the Government contract with Blackburn was ending and he began to look for another position. In August 1961, he had an interview with Bakelite in Birmingham and was offered a position in Research and Development. In September, he moved to Birmingham and stayed with his parents during the week, returning to Swanland at weekends. We put the house on the market for £2,900 (it had cost us £2,500) and we soon had a potential buyer. We decided to move to Coseley before the end of October, put the furniture in store and leave the house empty. This plan did not work out as we hoped because the buyers did not complete. We moved, nevertheless and went to stay with my mother. Little did we realise, in our naivety that empty houses do not sell well and it would be eleven months before we sold and were relieved of the mortgage and the storage costs. We were also paying bills at my mother's, I knew she would take any financial advantage that she could. I had brought my washing machine with me and she made sure that it had plenty of use and as ever her critical comments continued. Thankfully, Maude and Bertha kept away and I was kept afloat by going to see Keith's mother on Tuesdays and made friends with the local Baptist Minister's wife, Jean. She kept me sane, she had four children in as many years and was also the butt of my mother's snide remarks.

In June, we decide to book a holiday at Abersoch. We did not tell my mother until near to the time and as we expected she exploded again about us living beyond our means and much more. On the Friday prior to our departure, we learned that the house sale was going through and completion was days away, so our week in Abersoch with the children was a dream. Upon our return, my mother said that she wanted Keith to redecorate the hall and landing as part of the "wear and tear" of our stay. We did it and Keith's mother cared for the children. I had kept the garden and house in good order for her for eleven months, which is what she expected.

Chapter 13

We moved to a new modern house in Wootton Wawen on September 2nd 1962. We were an hour's drive from Coseley. It proved to be a very good move, the village was perfect for us and we joined in with much of what was on offer. We made friends quickly, the house was easy to organise and the garden adequate. At Christmas we bought a Staffordshire bull terrier puppy and also realised that we would be a family of five by August 1963. We did not tell anyone about the new baby because it seemed to us that it would be a long wait for Karen and Gail, they were aged three and two respectively.

On a visit to Coseley in March, having had tea with the family, it was Karen who announced "We are going to have a new baby." I will not repeat my mother's barking comments and again it was Fred who told her to stop it, or else. This was a strong message from Fred because he was a calm man. We waited a while until the dust settled and took the children home, dropping my mother off en-route.

Life in The Dale was very child orientated, almost every one of the 34 homes had children. There was a newly built village school, cricket ground, tennis courts and open spaces to meet friends. The village hall was old but adequate and we entertained children some afternoons during school holidays simply by playing games, crayoning and creating collages from magazines. On Wednesdays, we walked to Henley market to see the rabbits, goats, chickens and other livestock and were able to buy fresh vegetables and fruit to bring home in bags that hung from the pram. We also had our dog Ben to entertain us, he was a terror for cats and pet rabbits and he pestered the mobile butcher until satisfied with a large bone, which he gnawed for the rest of the day. We always seemed to have a houseful of visitors throughout the year, I think that the added attraction was nearby Stratford-upon-Avon!

1964. Our house in 'The Dale'. Very modern, all electric, open plan stairs, under floor heating. The worn out arms on the chair and one spindle leg of a slim TV can be seen. The girls are wearing jumpers knitted by Aunty Olive. They had at least two each year, one for their holidays and one for Christmas.

Our third daughter, Joann, was born at home on August 15th 1963. The dog was very much vigilant throughout the night and Karen and Gail awoke to welcome their new sister. We engaged a lovely lady from Bearley to come each day to help me. There were now five of us and a boisterous dog.

The mothers in The Dale were amazingly good with their support, we all knew what a little help was worth. As a form of light relief we started Wootton Wives where mothers could get together in the evening when the children were in bed. It developed into something quite special when we agreed to support mothers from the Ladywood area of Birmingham to enjoy time out together. It was all under the wing of the vicar of Ladywood, who had a fine reputation for his work in the community.

We raised money for a coach and the hire charge of Wootton Wawen village hall, so one day in the school holidays we entertained 35 children and a few helpers from their church to spend the day in Wootton. We arranged all kinds of activities plus a picnic lunch and afternoon tea. While the children were with us their mothers had some time to themselves. This happened for about eight years. I was also involved with the WI but found it difficult to attend all their meetings as they began at seven-thirty and I could not get three children settled in bed to enable me to change and leave the house by seven-fifteen.

Karen started at Wootton Wawen School in September 1964 and Gail followed a year later. It was convenient having the school so close as they went by themselves most days, stayed for lunch then Joann and I took the dog to meet them at the end of the day. We were so fortunate that it was a good school run by just two teachers, Mrs Rees the Headteacher and her deputy, Mrs Wilshaw. We enjoyed the birthday parties, school productions, sports days and outings, as well as the academic work. I was able to be at home and enjoyed caring for us all, even the troublesome dog. Regular visits were made to Coseley and we invited the grandparents and Aunty Olive to see everything in which the children took part. Keith's family were more than generous in providing expensive clothes, books and toys.

We now had a telephone which made communication easier, but my mother was now able to readily offer her advice and comments. She would buy a length of material from Cook's and tell me what to make, then for weeks after phone regularly to ask me if the job was finished. In an effort to pacify her, we invited her to stay with us on a Saturday evening after she finished work, Keith would drive to meet her in Birmingham and she would be with us before eight o'clock. These weekends were a nightmare. She never stopped telling us what she thought about the way we lived, then she would come to church with us and tell people (that she did not know) how wonderful we were, I could not believe what I was hearing. She went straight to work from Wootton on a Monday morning, Keith took her into Birmingham and she caught a bus to Dudley. After every visit, I was exhausted and relied on my friends to get me back on track.

One morning, when Karen and Gail were at school the Education Welfare Officer Mr Butterworth called and I invited him in. He advised me that I was a teacher and not working which amused me as I was working but not being paid! He asked me if I would consider tutoring a boy called Guy from Henley-in-Arden High School and after consideration, I agreed. So every Tuesday morning in term time, Guy cycled from Henley to receive an hour's tuition from me while Joann was happily playing in her bedroom. I never told my friends how much I was paid but it was more than one friend got for addressing envelopes at home for a week. Shortly afterwards Mr Butterworth called again to ask me to tutor a boy from Rowington School, this time I took Joann with me and the boy's mother entertained her, while I spent an hour with her son. To get to Rowington I borrowed a friend's mini-van while she was hair dressing at home.

I had a phone call from Henley High School one morning asking me to call and see the Headmaster so I made an appointment and walked to Henley, leaving Joann with a friend. I took with me all the progress reports for Guy, that I had sent monthly to Warwickshire Education Office. However, the Headmaster Mr Allen did not want to talk about Guy, he offered me a job on my terms, to start in September. I explained that Joann was not yet at school and he offered to get her into Wootton School earlier. I could not agree to this, I did not want to be offered any privileges, nor for Joann to be under any pressure. Mr Allen's next idea was to send Joann to the Montessori Nursery in Henley and for me to work around their opening hours, I agreed to do this. However, when Keith came home in the evening I told him of the plan and he was not happy for Joann to go to a nursery and when I thought about the implications I agreed that it was not in her best interests. The following morning, I phoned Mr Allen and told him that I was unable to accept his offer of a teaching post for September. He was so angry with me for withdrawing that I wrote to him and then let the matter rest.

When Joann went to school at Easter the following year, I contacted Mr Allen and he kindly offered me a part-time teaching post at Henley-in-Arden High School. There were now four teachers at the school, due to the extra children from The Dale. Several times, I had helped Mrs Rees when she was short staffed. In November 1967 I taught for six weeks 'on supply' to help Mrs Rees taking Joann with me. She was fully kitted out in surplus school uniform that had belonged to her sisters, she loved being in the Reception Class, even having a part in the Christmas production.

At Christmas, my mother gave each of the children a bracelet made from old silver three-penny bits, her sister Sally had given her the coins. These were the best gifts that she ever gave them but they had to keep thanking her, even when she spoke to them on the phone. I cannot begin to recall how many lovely, useful gifts their other grandparents and relatives gave them over the years, without having to express such reverence.

The money that I earned 'on supply' paid for a new carpet in the lounge and after Christmas I wasn't needed and happily returned to being a full time mum. Joann was so miserable not being able to return to school and continued to tell me that she could do the work, which she could. So for a few mornings a week she attended High View playgroup, run by Daphne Woodard, little did we realise High View would be put up for sale in October 1974 and we would buy it!

We were enjoying a very comfortable lifestyle. The only problem was with my mother, she was still falling out with everyone. The only consolation was that she enjoyed her position as the Millinery Buyer at Cooks, had an income from renting the factory warehouse and was well paid. She also had private commissions for special hats even though these hats made money for F.W Cook and not for her. Whenever she phoned she was abusive. She never had a good word to say about Keith, she never sent him a birthday card or gift at Christmas. It was hurtful, upsetting and cruel. The girls wrote notes to her, made gifts, phoned her and did all the things that grandchildren love to do. Keith's family were the exact opposite of my mother, they sent a package of sweets that arrived every Saturday without fail and when they came to see us, we went out for lunch, they always found an excuse to bring us a treat.

I learned to live with the embarrassment of a thrifty mother.

Chapter 14

In 1967 we went to an exhibition in London and chose a superb family tent and we now had an Austin Cambridge that easily carried us and the camping equipment. We enjoyed some good holidays even though we never experienced good camping weather. My grandma came to stay with us at The Dale and bought us a portable toilet to use with the tent, it was a blessing in disguise, we now could not fit everything in the car and had to acquire a small trailer. On reflection, camping was hard work but it enabled us to have holidays. My mother said that we were becoming like gypsies.

We saved hard and Keith's father was able to get us a magnificent Wolseley 1800 through British Leyland, for whom he worked. It was white with black leather upholstery and we drove to Coseley the following weekend and were so proud of the children and the car, we took everyone for a short ride. The following morning, when Keith had left for work, my mother rang and said, "Shirley, I have just rung Charles Clarke (a garage in Wolverhampton) you cannot afford that car. What does Keith think he is a Managing Director?" She was irate and I was in tears. I can remember saying that we had actually had to pay cash for the car because of the way we had acquired it through Fred but she was too angry to listen to me.

We went to the Long Mynd to pony trek at the end of May, using our new white car. It rained every day and the car had a muddy christening. Returning to Wootton, we decided that enough was enough, we valeted the five week old car and decide to sell the tent. It went to a colleague of Keith's at Bakelite, who also had three children.

Then we realised that we were without holiday facilities. My Aunt Lily came to the rescue and offered us a week at her house in Towyn, it was a delight and the weather was good. Then my mother came up with an idea, we could visit her sister Floss, who with her husband Percy, had recently retired to a bungalow in Bournemouth. She would arrange it. The previous year, Floss had sold her baby linen shop in Wellington, preparing to retire and my mother had suggested that we ought to go and get bargains for the girls. She and Floss created what seemed like a mountain of beautiful outfits for Karen, Gail and Joann. It was so tempting, especially as my mother encouraged me to have this and that as it would "come in handy". Floss gave me the bill, which I paid, as my mother smirked and coughed up not a penny. We left Wellington for Coseley where I dropped off my mother and drove to Tyseley to pick up Keith from work. I felt conned, my mother had tricked me into going simply to let Floss see that I had money and she had enjoyed a free outing. I could read her like a book.

Anyway, back to our holiday in Bournemouth with Percy and Floss. We collected my mother from Coseley and she stayed with us overnight in Wootton Wawen, then we left for Bournemouth the next day. Six of us arrived at Floss's two bedroom, immaculate home and were told that the children would be staying with another family close by. It was obvious to me that my mother had really worked hard on her sister to agree to put us up, she asked Floss and Percy if they liked our car, I was furious and convinced that this so-called holiday was to show off the children and the car. I counted the hours till our scheduled departure.

During the visit, I paid for the Sunday shoulder of lamb when we called at a butcher's, as Floss had gone to pay, my mother said "Leave it to Shirley" and Floss did as she was bid. When it was time to leave we said our farewells, gave little gifts to Floss, Percy and to the family who had had the girls and left. Stopping for fuel on the way home, my mother offered Keith a pound note. I was so thankful that he refused the money even though the mini break had cost us more than we could comfortably afford. It was yet another freebie for my mother.

However, we received splendid news upon our return; Karen had been offered a Direct Grant Scholarship to King's High School, Warwick, so we went out for a celebratory lunch. The following year, Gail won a similar offer at King's High School and a place at Stratford Grammar School for Girls, she chose the latter and off we went for another celebratory lunch. We now had two concerns, what would we do if Joann did not secure a grammar school place in three years time and what were we going to do about our holidays in the future? The answer seemed to be, save some money. Therefore, we did and we told our families of the plan.

As for holidays, we decided to hire a touring caravan. We set off for Derbyshire during October half term and all went well. In April 1971 we negotiated an overdraft to purchase a touring van from Allen's Caravans and within days set off for Cheddar in Somerset. Aunty Olive asked us if we were alright financially having made this purchase and Keith explained the situation and she lent us the money to save paying interest. We were grateful to her, it was not the first time she had helped us and we insisted upon repaying her on this occasion. We had many good holidays with the Europa 90 until we changed it in 1990 for a Compass Omega, which had all mod cons.

In 1974, Joann was offered a place at Stratford Grammar School and so we were in a comfortable situation, except for the continuous abuse from my mother. This led me to not telling her what we were doing, at times I had to lie in order to keep my sanity. We had saved hard to be able to pay for an Independent school for Joann had she not secured a grammar school place. If she had been offered a place at Henley-in-Arden High School, I would have looked for another teaching post.

Chapter 15

In October 1974 we realised that we were outgrowing The Dale and had another dilemma, we did not wish to leave Wootton as we were all so involved in village life. Keith was playing badminton at Henley-in-Arden and wanted to continue, he was also chairman of the club. The girls were all established in secondary schools, were in the church choir and also bellringers. I was on the Parish Council and Keith and I were busy with the village hall.

One evening, after playing snooker in the village hall, Doug Brown, told Keith that High View was on the market. We knew that it would suit us admirably. We went to see it, loved it and agreed to buy it. So in March 1975 we moved 200 yards across the road, we had more room and now lived next door to our friends the Browns, wonderful, nothing had to change. The dog was old and confused so regularly wandering back to howl outside number 15, we were continually retrieving him. When Ben died we decided not to have another dog.

There was only one person not happy about the move, my mother. She said we had "a millstone round our necks", if only she would appreciate that we were doing the best for our growing family and offered just a kind word but that was not in my mother's nature. Rose, Fred and Olive came to see us and brought house warming gifts as well as presents for the girls. This made me feel good yet sad that my own mother resented our happiness. I wondered what had damaged her so much in her formative years. I would never know.

In September 1975, I began to teach full time at Henley, we had much to do to the house and as the girls were now all in secondary schools, it seemed sensible and I enjoyed teaching. One day at school when speaking to the Educational Psychologist over lunch, she told me that they were extending their house to enable her elderly mother to live with them. My imagination went into overdrive... have your mother to live with you, impossible. Briefly I told her of

Keith and Shirley 1977 at High View.

my relationship with my mother, to which she replied, "It's your own fault." I was taken aback and she continued, "You should give her an ultimatum. Tell her to stop and change her ways or you get her out of your life for all time." Then she asked me what sort of nature Keith had and I told her that he was quiet, kind, loving and caring. To which she replied, "He must tell her to stop it." The bell rang for the afternoon session and I was left to think about a possible solution to a huge underlying situation. Keith and I did discuss the advice but it was easier said than done. It would have helped had I a brother or sister and we could have tackled her together. Maybe an opportunity would arise.

The girls did well at school and although Karen was not happy at Warwick, she battled on. Gail seemed to enjoy the social side of school, going most days with just a pen in her blazer pocket, Joann was the one that enjoyed school the most. Our family life was packed with activities, badminton, bell ringing, choir, pop concerts, as well as the usual family dramas. Keith and I were heavily committed to the old and new village hall and to some extent St Peter's Church and when the Revd Gordon Southeard asked if he could propose me for the Parish Council I agreed. This was probably because as a family we had been involved in 1971/2 with the village campaign to fight off the construction of an incinerator adjoining the sewerage works. We were both working full time, but as my mother so boldly told me, "Well, you are well paid, have loads of holidays and if I had had your chance, I would be on top of the world." Would nothing curb her bitterness? Keith and I did our best to keep our sadness to ourselves but as the girls grew older they began to read between the lines. This caused me considerable grief.

My grandma died in 1972 but we still had good relationships with my father's side of the family and went to see them as often as time allowed and they visited us at High View. There were problems when grandma's Will was known and my mother insisted that I ought to receive my father's share of the estate. The final settlements were delayed by many years. The lovely house in Webb Street was almost ruined by vandalism, having stood empty for so long, it also caused bitterness between the grandchildren.

My mother's behaviour was extraordinary. She would ring and say that a friend could bring her to Wootton for a day, knowing it would be during my half term. One day I received a phone call from the vicar of Coseley, he said that my mother had told him I would lead a walk around Wootton Wawen for their walking group, so could we fix a date? It all happened a month later. We led the walkers, they had a picnic lunch and returned to High View for tea in the garden. I had made the cakes and all my mother had to do was switch on the urn at two o'clock for our three o'clock return, all the cups were ready. Did she? No, she spent her time sitting with our neighbour Mrs Keyte and had forgotten, so we returned to no boiling water in the urn and had to resort to the kettle.

With three teenage daughters, our house was always busy. Colin and Margaret came for weekends in the summer and the five girls formed a five-a-side football team to play in a local league fixed by the Social Club. Sometimes there was a pig roast, all simple homemade fun. When the girls rang the bells on Sunday morning, the ringers came back to have coffee and marmite soldiers at High View, it was a busy household and we loved that.

The exam years were hectic with O and A Levels spreading from 1975 to 1981. The Parents' Evenings were not always positive but we plodded on, there was a life after school. I was also heavily involved with pupils at Henley, being on the other side of the table at Parents' meetings. However, we worked hard and played hard and it seemed to get us through. At the same time, we were attempting to get the girls through their driving tests.

Karen chose to go to The City of Worcester Training College and take a Degree in English with Drama and Dance. Taking her there in 1979 was like returning home for me, it was twenty-six years since I had been a student at Worcester. Gail did not enter the Sixth Form at the grammar school but chose to go to Stratford-upon-Avon College to obtain a BTec and A Level Law. Rather than go straight to university, she worked for a year at Henley Garage for Jimmy Leek and she so impressed him with her business skills, she could do no wrong in his eyes. He asked her to stay with the business but she went to read Accountancy at Bristol Polytechnic. Joann went into the Sixth Form at Shottery, took the Cambridge Entrance papers, but did not get an offer. She went to Manchester University and read Physics with a further year at St. Peter's College, Oxford.

In 1981 we had three spare bedrooms.

Chapter 16

In 1981 Colin and Margaret celebrated their Silver Wedding Anniversary with a party at St Chad's Church Hall. My mother was not invited and was bitter about being excluded, she insisted upon us calling to see her before we went to the celebration and we did. She was angry because she had made the head dresses for the wedding twenty-five years before and in her mind she deserved to be invited. This caused her to isolate herself from Keith's family, who had been so kind and generous to her for so many years, she behaved in an unbelievable way towards them and I was extremely embarrassed and upset. She never visited them again, thus missing so much. Even in later years when she knew that they had failing health, she never asked Keith how they were.

Fortunately, our daughters kept us involved with their lives and we were never at a loss for something to do. We made changes to our house and redecorated. We took on an allotment as well as all the other things we were doing when the girls were at home. For our first holiday alone together since our honeymoon, we went to Wells and Cheddar, calling to see our very old East Yorkshire friends, Pat and Chris who lived near to Devizes. It was their Silver Wedding weekend and we had been invited to join them.

During the years my mother did not give up on her harassment of me. She had never given anything to the girls during their student days and when I asked her why she replied "That's your job." One gift at Christmas was a jam jar with a painted lid, filled with cotton wool balls, her gift to me was a length of roller towelling, hand stitched. Her imagination never ran riot when it came to presents unless they were for her side of the family. My usual gift was a tea towel but on one occasion it was a second-hand necklace in an old watch box. We have nothing in our home that she bought especially for us.

In 1983 it was the year of our Silver Wedding Anniversary, our celebrations were cautiously planned knowing that the future of Bakelite was in jeopardy so a family party in the garden was felt to be the best thing to do. My mother asked if we intended to have a "bit of a do" and was told of the plan, her immediate reaction was to say "If Jack and Eileen are invited, I shall not come." In hindsight, I should have seized the moment and said "that's fine then, do not come" but as ever, her over powering manner reduced me to a wreck. The next day at church, I talked to Gordon Southeard, he listened and said, "Consider having a service on the Sunday, invite everyone to that and serve refreshments." It proved to be a pleasant occasion as friends from the village were able to join us.

On July 26th, we enjoyed an evening at The Porridge Pot in Warwick with Karen, Gail, Joann and Alan Heap, who at the time was Karen's friend. As a permanent reminder, we purchased a new sound system and the girls bought us a remarkable Postman's Clock, which we still have, ticking away in the lounge.

As anticipated, Bakelite was closed by BP in February 1985. On the very same day that Keith left Tyseley, our long-standing neighbour Denis was also made redundant from Dunlop, I think it was some consolation for them to have each other. It certainly gave Keith peace of mind finally putting Bakelite 'to rest', the past few years had been full of doubt, at least we knew where we were and could move on. My mother was, as always, quick to comment, "Ah, you never thought that it would come to this, him with no work." She stayed with us at Easter as she came every Bank Holiday because she insisted that we fetch her "it was our duty", we always had Good Friday together as a family and collected her on the Saturday.

Even her retirement day from F.W Cook's was a disaster. She was leaving on the Saturday and we went to Coseley to have lunch with Rose, Fred and Olive. At six o'clock we were waiting at the rear entrance of Cook's to meet her and take her back to Keith's parents', who had prepared a tea party to mark the occasion, so that we could all be together. She did not appear. We waited until a person whom I vaguely knew came out and I asked him if my mother would be long. He said that she had left early, as there had been a commotion. We drove to Ivy House Lane, finding her at home, distraught with anger. Apparently, something had upset her and she walked out early in a rage. This was on her retirement day! I could hardly look at her. After a while, she sorted herself out and we all went to have a delayed tea, nothing was said about retiring. It was a repeat of the evening when nothing was said about our engagement.

1983, the year of our Sliver Wedding. Joann, Karen, Keith, Shirley and Gail in High View garden.

The following Monday, her first day at home, her boss Mr Reginald Cook called to see her but she refused to open the door. He repeated the exercise for several days and still she refused to open the door. On his final visit, he left her an Indian hearthrug on the doorstep. My mother spent hours telling me this on the phone, she insisted that she had done nothing amiss and had given "her life" to Cook's. She never went to Dudley again.

Chapter 17

Having planted hundreds of trees with Denis in Austy Wood, Keith decided to set up on his own doing electrical work, he had taken time to decide his next move. He had been offered work in Aycliffe, County Durham when Bakelite closed but we considered all the options and decided to stay where we were. I had my post at Henley High School, Karen was in Birmingham, Gail in Bristol and Joann at Oxford.

Karen had completed her Degree at Worcester and had a PGCE from Birmingham Polytechnic. She was involved with lots of projects all to do with the Arts, she also lectured at Kidderminster College. Gail had done one year of her Accountancy Course at Bristol Polytechnic and she spent the summer vacation in Canada working, returned to Bristol unsettled and gave up the Accountancy Course. She remained in Bristol and within a short time established a thriving business making bespoke window drapes. Joann had completed her Physics degree at Manchester University and had embarked upon a PGCE Course at St Peter's College Oxford.

Keith did well within the village and had plenty of work without even advertising. Our income fell but we had invested redundancy payments and felt secure. Our biggest bonus was good health so Keith and I continued to give much time to village activities. We enjoyed caravan holidays with friends and on our own, continuing our policy of never going anywhere twice, the exception to this rule was the site at Eastnor Castle, close to Ledbury.

It was while I was secretary to St Peter's Church Council that I was reintroduced to Robert and Eve Baker, who I last saw when I was four years old. St Peter's had medieval wall paintings in the Lady Chapel and it was suggested that we approached the Eve Baker Trust to have them assessed and maybe restored. As secretary, I was asked to get in touch with the said trust. I could not say at the meeting that Eve Baker was my aunt, so the following afternoon I called at the vicarage and disclosed this information to Gordon Southeard. The same evening, I rang my mother to get Uncle Bob's address and I wrote to them, explaining who I was and waited for a reply. They rang me and it was a delight to speak to Eve, she was very keen to come to see the paintings so we arranged a date. Eve arrived, Gordon Southeard came from the vicarage and joined Keith and myself as Eve shot up the ladder, did what she had to do and promised a full report, adding "there will be no charge". Eve came back to our house and had lunch before returning to North Newington, as she left she said that she would be back and bring Uncle Bob. A few months later Eve and Bob came for lunch and after, we trooped to the church for him to view the paintings. They were good company, Bob gave me a hug as they left and said, "Thank goodness you are not like your mother." Eve kept her promise and sent a full report to the PCC, her advice was that the paintings were so badly broken up by memorial tablets that they were best left alone.

Sadly, Eve suffered from dementia just a few years after her visit to Wootton but we did see her one more time. Uncle Bob needed to sort out some paperwork and Aunt Floss decided that she and my mother would look after Eve while he, now living in the New Forest, would stay at home and concentrate upon his tax returns. I heard about this plan when my mother rang me and said that she wanted us to take her to Bournemouth the next weekend, which was a Bank Holiday and she would be there for ten days. I could not believe our luck, if we did this we would not have to have her with us. On the Wednesday evening we collected her from Coseley, returned to Wootton and drove to Bournemouth on Thursday morning.

We arrived in time for lunch. However, Bob was bringing the salmon and had not yet arrived, so we had coffee. We waited and waited, then began to think that we should go to a local pub for lunch. It was approaching three o'clock when Eve and Bob finally arrived! She was nothing like her former self and Bob had the salmon, it just had to be cooked! Keith and I made our polite excuses and left. We drove home and stopped to eat at a country pub.

The relief that we enjoyed as we opened the door and realised that for the first time in many years we were alone on August Bank Holiday. Saturday was lovely, there were no meals to cook. Then the phone rang in the afternoon, it was my mother.

"Shirley, I want you to come and fetch me. I want to come home."

I was deflated, "I will not," I said, "You have only been there for two days and you were staying for ten."

"Well, I want you to come and fetch me."

I flatly refused to fetch her as I did not want to drive on a Bank Holiday. She then put on her hysterical act and repeated the now well-used phrase, "It's your duty."

"I have done my duty by getting you to your sister's," I replied. The call went on and on, I suggested that she got a coach from Bournemouth to Wolverhampton or Stratford-upon-Avon which I would meet and then take her home.

"How old do you think I am? Travelling on a coach, I can't do that!"

She had broken me.

"What are you doing that you can't fetch me?"

"I am painting a window frame."

"What! If I had a man, you would not find me doing a job that he should be doing."

I was beside myself, would she never give up? Then telling me again that it was my duty, she put down the phone. I sat on the patio slabs and cried. Soon afterwards, Aunt Floss rang.

"Shirley, your mother wants to go home."

"Yes, I know and she needs you to get her a taxi to the coach station to board a coach to Stratford or Wolverhampton and I will get her home from there. I am not driving on a Bank Holiday." Floss ended the call.

Shortly after Joann rang from Manchester to tell me that she, Karen and Gail had all had their ears pierced that day, unbeknown to each other. Karen in Birmingham and Gail in Bristol. This made me smile because Keith had insisted that while under his roof, no ears should be abused. Joann realised that I was upset and asked what the matter was so I related the story. We chatted on as usual and finished our conversation.

Talking to Joann made me feel better and I made a pot of tea. Then there was another phone call, this time from Gail. She had heard the story from Joann and offered to help, she would leave Bristol at seven o'clock in the morning, which was Sunday and drive to Bournemouth, pick up my mother and return to Bristol for lunch. Keith and I would drive to Bristol and we would all have lunch together, then later in the afternoon we would drive her directly to Coseley and get her home. This plan worked well. My mother was preening, believing that she had won the day and in a way she had. She slept most of the time that we were driving on the M5 waking as we arrived at Kerwyn.

"There," she said, "that didn't take long did it?"

We ensured that she was safely installed in her home and drove to see Keith's family to receive a few words of consolation, before returning to Wootton. We did not have the patience to add up the mileage this escapade had taken, it was never mentioned again.

Chapter 18

My mother was approached by a builder to sell off the land upon which the factory stood. The premises had been empty for some time as the Auliffe brothers had moved, they had not surrendered the keys to her or paid rent for over two years and they still had materials on the site. I had spoken to my mother about the situation because it was depriving her of income, her response was that the Auliffes had been good to her and she was not going to ask for back rent of the factory. We were all aware that the Auliffes gave her a turkey every Christmas and she brought it to us.

My mother sold the land to a builder having had to have a mining survey completed to ensure that there were no pit shafts. We were aware of the survey but never saw it. She told me that she was going to give the girls something but not me, "You've got everything. You've had all the chances that I never had."

At Christmas, while on her usual visit, she gave Karen, Gail and Joann cheques for £250, with a stern warning not to waste the money that she had worked hard for and to remember that she had helped us when Keith's family could not. When all this was being said, Keith and I had gone to visit Mrs Keyte and Denis to take them Christmas gifts. The girls told us what had happened when we returned, my mother had even asked the girls if their father had any envelopes, when the reply was "Yes" she took three to use for the cheques! Her thriftiness knew no bounds.

My mother had helped us just once, by lending us £300 to put a deposit on The Dale, as we awaited the sale of Queensbury Way. I had delayed repaying her because of the way she had cheated me, using my Savings Certificates to pay for a wedding reception, not telling me about my father's Will and helping the Auliffes by under charging them rent. I should have had the confidence to challenge her but could not. Keith had wanted to repay her.

To celebrate my mother's 80th birthday in 1985, Keith and I took a complete buffet lunch together with a birthday cake to Coseley for her and her friends and she enjoyed a lovely gathering. She was happy and friendly all the time. To her friends, I was her amazing daughter, well educated through her sacrifices, with amazingly talented children, a husband with a good job (although at this point Keith was not working) and a lovely house in Wootton Wawen. When everyone left, Keith and I began the clearing and packing away and her mood reverted to what was her normal state with us and she reminded us that what we had done for her birthday was our duty. We drove home and realised that whatever we did was never going to please her.

Every summer holiday, my mother spent a few days with us, however in July 1988 I had a severe bout of sciatica two weeks before the end of term. When told about my incapacity she was very concerned about her holiday. I saw a specialist and did all that I could to get myself better. "When are you coming for me?" bleated my mother on the phone. There was no way that I could convince her that I was ill, housebound and restricted in every way. Keith spoke to her and told her the situation and we thought that had put an end to her pestering. At seven o'clock one morning she rang to tell us that she had a friend that would bring her to see me and they would arrive at about ten o'clock. Keith was now self-employed and decided to take a few hours off. On the dot of ten o'clock she arrived with a man from church.

"Why are you in bed at ten o'clock?" she asked.

Keith said, "Shirley is ill and you knew this."

"Could she not get up if she had a stick?" she insisted. Her reaction was unbelievable, my own mother had not believed me when I told her that I was ill. She was missing her stay with us and that was her grievance. She did not bring anything to cheer me up, not even a grape! Keith made sandwiches for lunch and our visitors left, they also left Keith with the clearing up. I was not well enough to return to school until November.

Joann taught at Henbury and then moved to London. She had renewed her friendship with Simon Letts, who she had known while he was at King Edward's School in Stratford and as a newly qualified Accountant, Simon was working for Touche Ross in London. Their friendship blossomed and after Simon had correctly asked Keith for Joann's hand in marriage, they became engaged and married at St Peter's Church, Wootton Wawen in August 1990. It was a totally home spun wedding which was their choice. We had a marquee, they walked to church and the family as well as friends in the village helped to create an amazing day, even the weather was perfect.

Months prior to the wedding, on one of our frequent trips to Coseley, we were at Kerwyn when my mother announced that she would come a few days beforehand and be with us to do any little sewing jobs. Keith reacted more quickly to this offer than I did and said that would not be necessary. So she took umbrage. Keith told her "We do not want you to cause any trouble, Alice." This was not what she wanted to hear. Then we called to see Rose, she was ill at home and would not be at the wedding. As the result of my mother's outrage, we did not see her after that until she attended the wedding on August 11th and it was a blessing in disguise. She was angry that Uncle Jack and Aunty Eileen were guests and could not believe that their grand daughter Caroline was bridesmaid. We were grateful to Mark and Caroline for escorting her back to Coseley.

For my mother's 90th birthday we paid for a garden makeover for her which would take three days by a couple of men. When I booked them, I said that we were paying for the rear garden only. When I went to see the finished work, I was told, "Your mother wants the front hedge clearing away." I paid them for the work I had agreed. "They've done a good job" said my mother, "but they haven't done the front hedge." I made a pot of tea and drove home.

The marquee that we had for Joann and Simon's wedding had left an impression upon us. To celebrate both our 60th birthdays in 1995 we repeated the party, albeit on a lesser scale. We had no intention of telling my mother and if she had heard via the grapevine, she never said anything. Having ruined our Silver Wedding Anniversary plans, she was not being given the opportunity to wreck this celebration. So one hundred people enjoyed supper together and the only thing that went wrong was that the entertainment failed to arrive... but that is another story.

Chapter 19

In February 1993, Karen married John Sackett at St Peter's Church, with the reception held at The Henley Hotel. My mother was invited and so was Fred but because of her animosity, she could not travel with Fred, Colin or Margaret even though it would have been more practical. She had not expressed any sympathy to Fred when Olive and Rose died. So Caroline and Mark took her there, then Keith and I took her back the same evening. "Well, you did your duty it went off well" she said as we left her at Kerwyn.

My mother was taken into the Corbett Hospital with a broken ankle, we went to visit her and she asked us to pay her electricity bill that was at home. Keith gave her £10 as she had no money, having left home in an emergency. I was upset when I read her hospital notes to see that she had given the name of Mrs Harvey as her next of kin. We paid the bill before our next visit to her. After several weeks, she was assessed and able to return home but would need her bed downstairs. Keith and I did what was necessary to make life comfortable for her homecoming, she would also have visiting carers.

Keith's mother had to go to a Nursing Home in 1991 and died in 1992. Aunty Olive died in 1991 so Fred was on his own but he soldiered on with the support of Colin and Margaret's family, Keith and myself. We visited him as often as we could and he came to stay with us at the time of the Wootton Wawen Allotments Show. We had a family lunch for him at The Dudley Arms to celebrate his 90th birthday in February but he died in April 1994. It was a sad loss and the end of an era. During all this time of grief, my mother never expressed any compassion.

In 1994, Gail and her partner Merlin left their home in Bristol and moved to Gisborne in Australia. Gail informed her customers that she would be back in two years and sent them notes to that effect. She had built a thriving business,

Keith with his father at 'The Dudley Arms' February 1994, Fred's 90th Birthday.

employed machinists, had obtained her private pilot's licence and had a dog, Tim, who after much deliberation she had flown out to Australia where he survived the long quarantine and enjoyed life in warmer climes. The idea of visiting Merlin and Gail in Australia, sowed the seed for me retire in July 1996.

By 1995, my mother needed more care at home and I managed to get her a Care Allowance so that she could pay for more help in the house. She was adamant that she did not want to go into a Care Home. Her longstanding and long suffering neighbours were amazing, doing her shopping, her hair and keeping her company, especially in the winter months. I phoned her regularly and we visited when we had the courage. She was still a powerful force.

When Aunt Bertha died in 1997, my mother rang to tell me and raged on again about how stupid she had been to pay in advance for her funeral and how it was going to be delayed because Roy Smout, Aunt Maude's eldest son, was abroad. This did not suit my mother either as he was "not flesh and blood", I was distraught by her bitterness and decided that enough was enough and the only way to express my feelings was by writing to her...

Tel: Henley-in-Arden
(01564) 792904

High View
Alcester Road
Wootton Wawen
Warwickshire B95 6BH

November 1997.

Dear Mom,

Since speaking to you yesterday, I feel that the only way forward, is to write. The uneasy situation between us has always been troublesome to me and a cause for concern.

When my father died, I tried my best at school and worked hard helping you run the home by doing the housework and tending the garden. This I did, when my friends were using their time, at leisure. However, whatever I did seemed to be taken for granted, indeed, a kind word would have been appreciated. You so often sided with your sisters when you should have supported my efforts. Your side of the family always took precedent. I recall a childhood of war, death and untold family squabbles, that upset me to this day.

The knowledge that my father had left me one hundred pounds in his will for the purchase of a piano, devastated me. I would have dearly loved to play an instrument. I find it difficult to believe that he instructed this and did not have the money for his will to be fulfilled – but if you say there was no money I am still prepared to believe you. Why were you not honest with me – I was, after all, only 12. For your husband's sake, why did you not tell the truth?

How can you ever expect me to forget the run-up to our engagement and wedding? Again with your sisters interferance? If you recall, I was off school when I taught

2

in Oldbury for six weeks_ with the skin problems that I was prone to - because of nerves. None of your sisters were worth inviting to our wedding, bar Aunt Lizzie - but they were and didn't have the courtesy to come. You still supported them.

Then came our beloved children. "I'm too young to be called granny, I'll be nana" - with your education I thought you would have known better"- "You're breeding like rabbits and will be in the gutter." I suppose I should have known your reaction to us having our family because I recall the words you said to me before I left for our wedding - "Don't get lumbered with a load of kids". It has all been so painful and I have tried my hardest to forget it - I can't. Perhaps you recall too saying - "It happened once between me and your father and you were the result". How sad. Without the support of Keith, the children, his family and our friends, I believe I would have broken.

We did our best to keep these incidents and many others away from the children, hoping that you would be able to bond with them. Sadly your criticisms continued and were totally unfounded about Rose, Fred and Olive. As the girls grew up, they understood for themselves. We have never tried to influence their judgements of you or anyone else. That would be unfair.

Our Silver Wedding plans were scrapped when you dictated that if we invited Jack and Eileen, then you would not come so - all was changed to have a family service followed by tea. I cannot think why we were so tolerant of your demands but in those days, we were.

3.

Why were you able to give Bertha a beautifully framed picture of the paintings in Wood Green village hall and the same year give me for a Christmas present, a second hand necklace in an old watch box? It really tells me what your priorities are.

We always gave you the best hospitality and presents that we could afford. We funded your 80th birthday as well as the garden restoration for your 90th. If you sit down, you will recall the other presents too. But that is not what it is really all about. Your unfairness has been very hurtful.

When you were in the Corbett Hospital in May/June 1996 you asked us to pay your telephone bill, which we did.

Prior to you coming home, we went to your house to move the single bed downstairs. To my shock and horror, we found a lot of cash in a red wallet. It was far too much to be in a house but I know you left home in an emergency. Why did you not have sufficient confidence in us to say "There is money at my house, pay the 'phone bill from it and put the rest somewhere safe". This could have been either put in the bank or we could have held it until you came home. Oh no, you would not be so trusting – but rather risk it be stolen.

Perhaps it was wrong, but when looking for the sheets for your single bed, I found your will and I read it.

I am delighted that you have left your house and effects to the girls. What I cannot credit is the fact that Mr Field along with Karen are your Executors. Currently you are highly critical of Mr and Mrs Field – who I think are untold good to you – but you have empowered him to be in charge

4.

of your final wishes. As your only child, I have no right to enter your house, my home as a child, in the event of your death. I find this shattering.

I have thought long and hard before expressing my thoughts to you on paper. No doubt you feel that I have been unfair to you. I am prepared to talk all of this, and more over with you in the presence of a third person of your choice.

I hope that you will re-read this carefully as I have written it straight from my heart – as for our future, I do not know what else I can do, because sadly you have pushed me to my limit.

Yours so sadly,

Shirley.

I gave copies to Karen, Gail and Joann, knowing that it could affect their inheritance. I attended Bertha's funeral but felt no sadness. I met my cousin Phyllis at the service whom I had not seen since I was a teenager, she was delightful and we have enjoyed several other days with each other since.

My mother received the letter on a Saturday, deliberately, I knew that she would have her friend with her as was the usual practice. At seven o'clock in the morning our phone rang and I was called everything imaginable from callous and wicked to selfish, greedy and more. I could not get a word in but held onto the phone until she rang off. I sat on the bed and cried. Later in the morning, I had a call from the Revd Matthew Baynes, vicar of Christ Church in Coseley to tell me that he was with my mother and she was very upset that I had sent her a letter that was all lies. I asked him if he had read it, to which he replied that he had not because my mother had burnt it. I rang him back and read the letter to him. He was speechless.

A few days later, Matthew Baynes rang asking if I would meet him at Kerwyn to resolve the problem. We agreed a date. I deliberately wore a suit that my mother had seen before and arrived on time at nine-thirty in the morning. The vicar opened the door and revealed my mother seated on the settee, well dressed with full makeup and jewellery. The sun was shining and the sitting room looked lovely.

"Oh my god! You look ten years older than when I last saw you" she said as I sat down.

"Now," said the vicar, "tell me Shirley, what do you want of your mother? How can we make amends?"

"Just the truth and a kind word," I replied. The vicar was seeing this regular churchgoer, who wore her splendid array of hats while sitting in the same pew, week after week in a very different light.

"Shirley have you one question to ask your mother so that we may find common ground?"

"Yes. Mom, why do you not have any wedding photographs?"

"You little madam! We were too poor."

I responded, "You were too poor, Dad always ran a car as well as a van for his business and you were able to buy a house and the adjoining land when you married in 1933. Then Dad built the veranda, landscaped the garden with natural stone and you gave birth to me in a private nursing home. You owned a camera, had holidays and started a collection of Stourbridge cut glass. How could you be poor?"

CHAPTER 19

Turning to the Revd Baynes I said, "Now do you understand our problem?" My mother began to cry. There was nothing that could be salvaged from this sad situation. It was too late. I left the house that had been my miserable home, got to my car and realised that I had left my glasses behind. Could I risk driving home without them and just get another pair? I pulled myself together and decided that it was a foolish idea so I went back and rang the bell. The vicar opened the door and I explained the reason for my return. My mother perked up, "I knew you'd come back!" I ignored her, found my glasses on the chair and left for a second time. In my head I could hear her saying, "It's bad luck to turn back" which made me drive very carefully with a song in my heart. I decided that I never wanted see her again.

Once home, I wrote immediately to the Revd Baynes thanking him for trying to help me. Before I had even finished the letter, he rang me to say how worried he had been about me driving on the motorway. I assured him that I had sung all the way to Wootton. He then said that what he had witnessed between my mother and I was unimaginable, he had seen her in a very different way.

The Parish of Coseley
Christ Church with St. Cuthbert's

The Revd Matthew TC Baynes (Vicar)
The Vicarage
Church Road
Coseley
West Midlands

11th December 1997

Dear Mrs Davies,

Thank you for your letter which I received at the weekend. Since then I have been to see your mother again and have tried to express to her how you are feeling. I have to say I don't really think we made very much progress. As I am sure you are only too well aware, she has an amazing ability to blank out what she doesn't want to hear. The destruction of the letter you sent was in a sense quite a symbolic action in terms of the way she chooses to deal with things in life that she doesn't want to face. She is clearly very distressed by what has happened, and by the breakdown of the relationship with you, but does not really see that she is in any sense culpable for what has happened. To Alice everything comes down to £. s. d. and she is convinced that your unhappiness with her stems from having discovered the contents of her will. She refers to loans made to your family many years ago, turkeys supplied at Christmas etc. etc. it all comes back to money. She does not seem able to understand that money for you is not the issue, but that her "thriftiness" with her finances over many years, has been a justification for a meanness of spirit and lack of trust. I suspect that much of her anger, and that is what her actions are prompted by, is rooted in a poor relationship with your father. I wonder if she ever really forgave him for leaving her on her own, and with you to look after.

I have to say that so deep rooted is all of this that I suspect that trying to tackle it now is just too late. To be honest this should have been dealt with many years ago, at a time when perhaps she might have been able to find some peace within herself, and with you. I think that unlikely now. I am deeply sorry for you, and recognise the pain you must have felt all these years. I truly understand how you might use the word "abuse" to describe the nature of the relationship which you must have endured with you mother. At times it must have felt like that, although I suspect in a strange way your mother always believed that what she was doing was best for you.

As to the future I am not sure that I have any advice to give. You say in you letter that I should "let you know if you can be of any help." I must say in reply to that, and in order to clarify my position, that I am here to help and assist you and your mother, it is not a case of what you can do to help me. Despite all the pain and the suffering she may have caused you over the years I don't think responsibility can be abandoned at this stage. Even if the relationship with you mother is not one that can be salvaged then I still believe that there is a duty to ensure that she is cared for, even if that is conducted through the medium of the social services. I know that may sound hard, but I actually believe that it is in the interests of your own peace of mind as well, if that is recognised. Your mother is not going to be with us for a vast period of time, and I think that having seen it through for as long as you have, and to be sure that you can ultimately lay all the pain to rest, you need to see it through to the end. I suspect that is not what you may want to hear, but I write believing that to be true, and I am not attempting to "guilt trip" you back into relationship with your mother.

As I have said to you before I am here to help, and am more than happy to be a third party if and when you and your mother choose to meet again. The initiative for that meeting though will need to come from one or other of you. I have suggested to Alice that she pick up the phone, but I suspect that such a gesture is probably beyond her, and will need to come from you.

As to Christmas it is my understanding that she will be going to her niece (presumably your cousin) as she did last year.

I am sorry if this letter brings you further grief, but I thought it best to write to you honestly as I see the situation.

Yours sincerely,

Matthew T. C. Baynes

After a wonderful career at Henley-in-Arden High School, I retired in July 1996 having taught there for twenty-nine and a half years. In October, Keith and I went to see Gail and Merlin in Australia, staying for seven weeks. We visited amazing places and the sunshine was an added bonus.

As a family we rented a house in Derbyshire for Christmas 1996, it was the first Christmas without my mother, she went to her niece Brenda who lived at Woodcross. There were ten of us, Karen, John, Melanie and Zoe, Simon, Joann, Basil and Fennel, Keith and me. Caroline and Eve came to visit for a day.

In January 1997, I really began to enjoy my days at home, although I was called in by the High School to help with supply teaching on several occasions. Keith and I caught up with jobs, enjoyed caravanning holidays, entertaining at home and visiting our family. Simon and Joann had Basil and Fennel and included us in much of what they did, they moved from Cricklewood to Letchmore Heath.

John and Karen had Melanie while living in Birmingham and Zoe while in Glasgow. Sadly, their marriage ended and Karen returned to Birmingham with the children, we were much involved, helping whenever we could and loved to do so. We went to Australia every other year to see Gail. Eventually Merlin went to work in America whilst Gail remained in Australia. Later Gail married Leo but sadly, that did not last.

Chapter 20

In January 2003 I made an appointment to see the vicar of Coseley, the Revd Heather Humphries who was now the new incumbent. I had not seen my mother for six years and she was now in her 98th year. Karen had kindly taken on the role of next of kin in spite of all her other commitments and I was grateful to her, but felt guilty. As a family we had discussed in advance the funeral arrangements for my mother and I had written them down for the vicar. She was sympathetic and honest with me that my mother had caused her concern, she would not receive Communion from her and had refused to say the Lord's Prayer on occasions when the vicar had visited her in hospital. I was not surprised to hear these words and confided in the Revd about our relationship, I felt that my hour with her was extremely fruitful.

Karen took the children to see my mother several times, taking suitable food for their meal as they were still very young, I admired Karen for doing this when she already had so much to do by herself. On one such visit my mother gave Karen a very old coat (size 18) and the children 50p, in the circumstances it broke my heart, Karen's life was sad enough at the time and she did not need her to behave like this.

My mother was admitted to Russells Hall Hospital in Dudley after having had a fall. Karen and I met at Ivy House Lane to ensure that the property was safely secured. We emptied away the perishable foods and generally tidied up, changed the bed linen and left everywhere looking neat. We were amazed to find a red leatherette wallet in the sideboard containing almost £5,000. We left with the money and called at Tesco in Dudley for a quick lunch, who would believe that we had so much cash in a plastic bag? Keith transferred the money into my mother's account in Sedgley. Later when she was discharged from hospital, she had more care and Meals on Wheels but she refused to pay for the food, saying that she knew people who had it for free. She struggled on, fiercely independent. She never rang me. Her friends did and told me how ashamed I should be. The carers changed frequently because she upset them and on one occasion I wrote to Dudley Social Services and apologised on her behalf, she would never apologise. Her neighbours were golden and I still feel indebted to them eleven years after her death.

Early in January 2004, I received a call from Russells Hall Hospital and was advised that my mother was seriously ill, she had been admitted following another fall at home. They apologised for phoning me but they could not reach Karen. A doctor spoke to me and said that they had resuscitated my mother three times and what were my wishes? Thanking the doctor, I said "Please let her go, she has had an extraordinary long life." Two hours later, the Bereavement Officer called to tell me that my mother had died.

I was unaffected. My friends had said that I would be filled with grief and remorse when she died. I was not. The following day, Keith and I went to the hospital, collected the death certificate and personal belongings before driving to Hartlands, the Undertaker's in Hurst Hill. Frustrated by the slow speed of the clerk, I filled in the oversized pink form myself, we refused the tea and pleasantries and discussed the arrangements for her cremation.

It took a while to find a clergyman to carry out the service, it had to be someone who did not know her and certainly I could not ask the Revd Humphries for whom my mother had no respect. The cremation would be early in the morning and private with only Karen and Joann, her granddaughters present. We only needed a hearse and all was arranged before we left for Australia the following Tuesday.

I received a phone call on the Sunday evening from Hartlands informing me that the day and time of the cremation had leaked out in Coseley. Knowing that we had not told Colin or Margaret any details of the cremation in order to protect them from hassle, the information must have leaked from the undertakers. I gave Hartlands Karen's phone number and advised them to reschedule the cremation. Karen negotiated with Joann and it was done.

We rang Karen from Australia on the day of the cremation to see if all had gone to plan. It had. We later learned that the Revd Humphries had given my cousin Bertha, Karen's telephone number without consent even though she was aware of the family problems. Karen had had to listen to a torrent of abuse from

Bertha, including the accusation that her grandfather had died from syphilis, a most wicked thing to say to someone that you had never met and also not true. Karen rang Colin, her Godfather for support.

We returned from Australia and it took me a while to appreciate that I would no longer be verbally or mentally abused again.

Karen, Gail and Joann inherited my mother's house. It was put onto the market and there was immediate interest. However, the house held a deep secret that prevented it from ever being lived in again. Beneath its foundations, were two deep pit shafts that had been capped in 1903. By the 1980s the iron plates had corroded and the house began to slowly sink. When my mother died at the age of 99, there was nothing that could be done to salvage the property and it was taken down brick by brick by contractors employed by The Coal Board. The vacant plot may be seen today in Ivy House Lane, Coseley. The house always had a sinister feel and I shudder to think about the days that I lived in it.

Some parishioners of Christ Church did have a memorial service for my mother.

How do I know? They sent me the service sheet, anonymously.